Casey Donovan: Blond Bombshell

Gay Porn's Pioneering Megastar

David Bret

DbBooks

Copyright © 2017 David Bret

ISBN: 978-1546388180

A catalogue record for this book is available from the British Library.

This book is dedicated to the memory of Casey Donovan (1943-87), a true *Enfant de novembre*, and to Wakefield Poole for giving him to the world.

"N'oubliez pas…la vie sans amis c'est comme un jardin sans fleurs

Contents

Introduction

I think my greatest accomplishment so far is something that doesn't show up in lights or get reviewed - and that's simply the sexual sanity that I have tried to contribute to over the last twenty years.

This was Casey Donovan, speaking in an interview in 1983, four years before his timely death.

He was a pioneer, and along with a mere handful of others will eternally remain amongst the elite of the adult film industry, the cream of the crop. Like Joey Stefano, his nearest equivalent of the next generation and also the subject of a biography by this author, he was a Janus figure, a complex individual not always easy to define. Away from the studio, inasmuch as Joey became Nick Iacona, his birth name, so Casey Donovan was always Calvin Culver. The two were always separated: the porn superstar and the boy-next-door. Like Joey, nothing was too exhibitionist or outrageous for Casey to do on the screen, while away from the studio he is known to have been shy and unassuming. On the screen he could be smug and aggressive, but it was all part of the act—what the director demanded. Though inordinately handsome, having a partner who was thus was not always essential for Casey, proving to the viewer that even an unattractive man could "pull" someone who looked like a Greek god. It was all make-believe, but it invariably worked.
This is his amazing story…

1: Cal

I really have this incredible morality....very prim and upright underneath, yet I've gone off the deep end and frequently done all kind of things. I must be a Doctor Jekyll and Mr. Hyde sort of person. (Casey)

He was born John Calvin Culver on 2 November 1943, in East Bloomfield—a small community in New York's Ontario County. His parents, Donald and Arlene, lived on a farmstead and there was an elder brother, Duane, born in 1936. No one ever addressed him as John: it was always Cal.

Little is known of Cal's childhood other than what he recalled about himself. When the war ended in Europe and US servicemen began coming home, the Culvers did their bit to help, turning their home into a motel, and transforming part of the farm into a camping and caravan park. The move was popular with holidaymakers on a budget, and who could not afford the steeper prices at nearby Canandaigua, a popular holiday resort, but condemned by the locals, many of whom were Spiritualists and Mormons and who took exception to "liberal-minded" tourists—in other words, "swingers"—invading their sedate puritanical environment.

The recollections of friends and acquaintances—speaking in retrospect and juxtaposing callow farm-boy Cal Culver with the porn star he became—may be fictitious, or at least greatly embellished. In his biography, Roger Edmonson places asterisks before the names of men who claim to have known Casey intimately, requisite to retaining their anonymity. Many of these stories come across as highly-elaborated exercises in wishful thinking, and must therefore be taken with a liberal pinch of salt. Reading so many of them, one might conclude that if Casey Donovan *did* have this much sex during his short life, there would have been little time left for eating and sleeping. It was as if these people *had* to say something scandalous about him because of who he became, whether it was true or not.

Thus we are told that the teenage Cal acquired a sexual awakening when, as part of his duties in the caravan park, his parents assigned him to cleaning the men's shower-blocks. One story claims that he realized that he was gay, pre-puberty in 1955—the year his brother Duane left high school to join the military—while watching men showering without bothering to close the partitions separating the cubicles. Another states that once he became sexually active he cruised for sex around the caravan park, mostly with straight men, and took these back to the shower-block so that he could allow friends to spy on the action through a knot-hole in the next wall. Suffice to say, when holding nothing back in an interview with Allan Leopold of *In Touch*, in July 1974, he mentioned nothing about this, which may be enough to suggest that his sex life thus far had progressed no further than a spot of voyeurism—that *he* was the one watching with his friends, and not a participant.

Cal was enrolled at the Canandaigua Academy in September 1957, and proved popular both with the teachers and other students on account of his sunny, outgoing disposition. During his second year he attended drama classes, and formed a close bond with his English mistress, Helen Van Fleet. Indeed, he often said that she was more of a mother to him than his real mother, and the two became friends for life. Helen—he called her "Aunty Mame" while she baptized him "Patrick", after the characters in the 1958 film—appears to have been made aware of his sexuality early on during their friendship, and to have accepted this and supported him. Under her tutelage, he joined the Academy Players, the school's amateur dramatics group. He also worked in the library, part-edited the school's newspaper *The Cannon* and was appointed his class's secretary and treasurer.

What is strange, given the puritanical beliefs of those around him, is that there is no record of Cal ever being subjected to homophobic prejudice. He never hid his light under a bushel. He was always openly gay, even to his parents—and if his father disapproved, his mother apparently did not. While other boys in his year aspired to joining the school football team, Cal was only interested in being their cheerleader, a brave step for a young man to take. And though everyone at school knew that he was gay *and* dating men after class, this did not stop the girls from pursuing him, resulting in him dating a few of these as well—for no other reason, he later said, than he loved ballroom dancing, which might be frowned upon should he turn up at the local dance-hall and execute the tango with another boy!

If Cal was not interested in football and some of the "rougher" sports, he was passionate about gymnastics, in particular the vaulting horse, and the parallel bars. This saw him visiting the gym on a regular basis, and ultimately led to him acquiring the physique which in later years made audiences swoon with envy. Yet when he graduated during the summer of 1961, it was not to an acting or sporting career that he aspired—but in following in the footsteps of his surrogate mother, Helen Van Fleet, and becoming a teacher.

Cal enrolled at the S.U.N.Y. teaching college in Geneseo, a small establishment with 1,000 students, where he joined the Phi Sigma Epsilon Fraternity and the school's choir. The Glee Club appointed him their president. As with his previous school, when asked to join the football team—standing 5 feet 10 inches and tipping the scales at a sporting 155 pounds, he was considered the perfect specimen —he chose to become their cheerleader. He played major roles in every production that took place while he was an alumnus: *Little Mary Sunshine*, *Bye Bye Birdie* and Peter Shaffer's *Private Ear* were but three, and danced in *The Pajama Game*.

Living close to Rochester enabled Cal to visit the Eastman School of Music, home to the Rochester Philharmonic Orchestra, and to attend as many of their concerts as he could. To finance these trips, he got a job in the college canteen. He appears to have had sex for the first time, negating the tall tales of his supposed activities in the shower-blocks back at home. It was two days before the college's Hell Week, but he was not allowed to participate in the activities after being laid low with a slight case of mononucleosis and suffering a nose bleed. Some years later, speaking to the journalist Allan Leopold, he recalled what happened:

9

Instead, I went to the country with my math professor. He was a gorgeous guy, about thirty-three, with salt-and-pepper hair and he owned a smashing ultra-modern farmhouse. I had to be back at 6:30 the next morning to work in the cafeteria and I was green as grass. He got me a little high and we went upstairs together. He pointed to the guest room and said, "You can sleep in there or in here with me." I mumbled some dumb think like, "Oh, I don't want to mess up another bed." We were lying there in the dark and my heart was just pounding away. I could hardly control my breathing. He rolled over on his stomach and flung his arm across my chest. He whispered, "I hope you don't mind?" Suddenly we were kissing. I gasped, "You know, you're the first guy I've ever been to bed with." He said, "You don't kiss like it." **[1]**

Cal appears to have been the active partner on this occasion, something which he said changed, three weeks later in New York, when he made eye-to-eye contact with a man leaning against a car:

I was wearing my penny loafers, button-down shirt, skinny tie, Madras jacket and short hair. The whole bit I was really square and ready for anything. This guy taught me everything. When my virginity went, I thought, "Never again!" God, it hurt for days and it was literally months before it happened again. **[2]**

10

Photographs taken at the time reveal Cal as not looking in the least like the regular hustler. He never wore leather, contour-hugging T-shirts or vests, or bulge-revealing shorts like other hustlers. Rather he always dressed immaculately in tweed jackets, neatly-pressed trousers, designer shirts and shoes, and was rarely seen in public without a tie. Of his passion for sparing no expense when it came to looking good when cruising, he confessed:

> *I always splurge. I'm so profligate with money. But it gives me such a good feeling to buy something terribly expensive that I love and just show it off. I bought this super Safari jacket at Saks and plunked down a hundred bucks for it. These black patent leather loafers are Gucci, and the hairdo is Sassoon. I also had a manicure, and before I was through I had gone through $250. Bills are always hanging over my head but, like Mame, I want to live!* [3]

It is very likely that this man, thought to have been a doctor, had seen Cal in one of the cruising areas, otherwise he would not have risked propositioning him in the street, and in broad daylight. London had Hampstead Heath, Paris the Bois de Boulogne—and New York had the Rambles, a gay cruising area in Central Park. In 1964, New York was the venue for the World's Fair, when more and more gay venues found themselves raided by the police on account of Mayor Lindsey's recently-introduced clean-up campaign, to such an extent that they were closing at an alarming rate. Areas such as the Rambles were

11

therefore essential places for gay men to meet—not always for actual sex, but to hook up and repair to somewhere less risky. For those who did want to take the risk, and there were many who found sex more exciting this way, like London and Paris the cruising areas had their own particular "policing" system. Sometimes this was a member of the gay community, occasionally a friendly police officer who, at the end of his shift would be suitably and sexually rewarded for keeping an eye out for the vice squad. He would blow a whistle if danger was imminent so that those having fun in the bushes could make a getaway. Cal was one of the gutsier cruisers and so far as is known was never caught.

In the spring of 1965, 21-year-old Cal graduated from Geneseo with a BS in elementary education, and acquired a position teaching mathematics and history to sixth-graders in Peekskill, in New York's Westchester County. It was only now that he found his niche in society, when he spread his wings and began driving into New York. With his innate charm he quickly became the darling of the theatrical set when he began frequenting the theatres on and off-Broadway, and because he was always smartly dressed he was often mistaken for someone of importance and allowed to mingle backstage with the actors and directors. He also developed a fervent interest in museums and art galleries.

Cal's staid social life in Peekskill could not possibly compare with the hedonistic delights of New York's seamier side, once he had sampled this, and Cal opted to spread his wings a little further. He left Peekskill and took a position at the Ethical Culture Fieldston School, a private establishment in

Central Park West whose alumni included a great many children of celebrities and wealthy business people. This he felt would complement his standing with the theatrical set, until he found out—to his chagrin—that many of these were over-privileged, spoilt brats. One incident involved the daughter of the actor Eli Wallach, who allegedly made the teachers' lives a misery until Cal opted to teach her a lesson by giving her a kick up the backside. Wallach complained to the principal and he was given his marching orders. Recalling the incident, however, he does not appear to have held a grudge against her:

> *Harry Belafonte's kids, Steve Lawrence and Edie Gorme's kids, Eli Wallach and Anne Jackson's kids. My favourite student was Roberta Wallach. I saw where she was just in the film* The Effect of Gamma Rays on Man-in-the-Moon Marigolds. *Isn't that neat? Roberta and I becoming stars at the same time. Who would have thought, six years ago?* **[4]**

This incident with the doctor encouraged Cal to re-invent himself as a new kind of hustler, one who no longer frequented potentially dangerous hunting grounds late at night, but plied his "trade" in more respectable locations—museums, art galleries, hotel lobbies, and exclusive eateries. It was by way of a client that he met in one of these establishments that he acquired an audition for the kind of work he had always wanted to do—acting in summer stock. He was taken on by the Peterborough Players, based in

Hampton, New Hampshire, where as a member of the New London Barn Playhouse he soon learned that stars were not made overnight. He remembered his summer in Hampton as the best in his life so far:

> *I cleaned toilets, constructed and painted sets in exchange for free room and board. I had a part in Tennessee Williams'* The Night of the Iguana *and I was featured dancer in* Funny Girl, Annie Get Your Gun, Oliver *and* The Student Prince. *I also met my lover, Donald, there. He returned to New York with me and moved right in.* [5]

Cal introduced Donald to his mother, who seems to have approved of their relationship, though he made it clear to his lover from the offset that he would never be monogamous. Indeed, variety would always be the spice of his life, no matter who he was involved with, and future lovers would just have to accept this. He was still mixing with the rich and famous, for even some of the biggest names liked to take a step back and perform in smaller venues like the New London Barn Playhouse between Broadway productions. Also, a substantial number of these were gay or at least bisexual, and unable to resist the charms of this ever-smiling young hunk—and willing to pay handsomely for a few hours of his company.

One man that he and Donald met during their travels was the former tough guy actor Tom Tryon, now starting to make his name as a best-selling novelist. And if Tryon made little or no impression on Cal then, he soon would, as will be seen.

Upon his return to New York, Cal successfully auditioned for a small part in Harold Rome's off-Broadway production of the musical-comedy, *Pins & Needles,* which had opened at the Roundabout Theatre on 19 May 1967, and which ran for 214 performances. He was not paid much, and augmented his income by taking any number of ad-hoc jobs. He waited on at Serendipity 3, the exclusive celebrity restaurant, where amongst those he served were Jackie Kennedy, and Andy Warhol muse Holly Woodlawn who became a friend. Over the Christmas and New Year period, Cartier's employed him as their doorman where even his immaculate tweeds were not smart enough and he was supplied with a Pierre Cardin wardrobe which drew closeted gay clients towards him like a magnet. He recalled one amusing incident:

Liz and Richard were in town and she had sent over her big ring to be polished. Well, I just had to go upstairs and look at it. And you can print that I wore Liz's diamond. I slipped it on my finger and I know now why she was devoted to Burton. My dears, it was as big as a peach pit! [6]

In February 1968, Cal embarked on a "hustler's travel-a-thon" which courtesy of a succession of wealthy clients saw him covering thousands of miles, and rubbing shoulders with actors, movie stars, entrepreneurs, and even royalty. This kicked off, according to an interview he gave, when he sailed to Hawaii "with a credit card and $70", worked as a busboy in Waikiki, loved it, and had his first threesome there. He adds that he lived on $1.05

15

a day and never overshot his budget because, everywhere he went, people took him in:

> *That September I went off on my super adventure. I sailed on the* S.S. France *for London, Paris, Brussels and Amsterdam all by myself....I saw the opening of Nureyev's* Nutcracker Suite *in Covent Garden. In Brussels I saw* Man *of la* Mancha *with Jacques Brel and Joan Diener, sung completely in French. I did the Canal Tour in Amsterdam and all that sex went to waste because I didn't know my way around. However, last October I made up for all that. I found the gayest hotel there. I ran out of money, sailed for home, found a rich lover and sailed right back to London. Then on to Kenya. We stayed near Mombassa for two weeks and we never got out of bed. A few months later I went to Spain. In Torremolinos, I found the most marvelous Spaniard who turned out to be an American from Boston...* [7]

Back in New York, Cal received a call to audition for the Wilhelmina Agency, founded the previous year by the Dutch model, Wilhelmina (Gertrude Behmenburg 1939-80) and her husband, Bruce Cooper who was the executive producer of *The Johnny Carson Show*. During the 1950s and 1960s she was one of the world's most celebrated models, appearing on the covers of over 200 magazines—28 times for *Vogue*. Discerning, she took to Cal at once and hired him on a salary of $60 an hour, a tidy sum

16

for the day. Over the coming months his face would appear in ads in Sunday supplements, mail-order fashion and underwear catalogues, and on covers of romantic novels. He made his first pornographic loops at this time, of which nothing is known other than they were heterosexual and that the women in were paid considerably more than he was:

> *I did porno strictly for the money and begun with a bunch of sex reels for sleazy 42nd street grind houses that sold under the aegis of sex education lectures. They had titles like* Doctor X *and* Twin Beds. **[8]**

On 19 October 1969, Cal returned to the stage in David Gaard's drama, *And Puppy Dog Tails*, at New York's Bouwerie Lane Theatre. Directed by Michael Devereaux, this was one of the numerous independent all-gay productions which sprang up in the wake of the Stonewall riots the previous June. It was one of the highest-grossing productions of the winter season. Cal understudied Edward Dunn, but as Dunn was indisposed regularly during the 141-performance run, Cal was able to show audiences what he was made of. The story centered around devoted lovers John and Carey-Lee, whose East Side love-nest is thrown into chaos when they enter into a love-triangle with Bud, a straight man they pick up. There were several nude scenes. Ruben Burrero observed in *Homosexual Renaissance*:

> *And Puppy Dog Tails* is a delightful off-Broadway experience, hilarious and heartwarming. It is a play about people who

17

feel they can achieve happiness only as homosexuals. It is *not* a simple display of nudity, nor a play *just* for homosexuals. Nor is it a convention of commiserating queens, so called so that society might have a feast of stereotyped attitudes on homosexuals. Bud cannot understand the relationship that John and Carey-Lee have built. He misunderstands the ideal of true happiness, for he cannot see beyond his own fears and the inhuman attitudes of Western society. He unconsciously sins against the life-force of human love, which has left his soul crippled and unable ever to know love of any kind. **[9]**

The play closed on 7 January 1970. Cal auditioned for the part of Rodney Allworth in the low-budget sexploitation spy movie, *Ginger*, which if nothing else certainly fits into the so-bad-it's-good category. He recalled:

> *I had no idea what kind of picture I was getting myself into. To audition for it, I decided to dress the part of the elegant movie star. I showed up for the reading in my double-breasted blue blazer, my Pierre Cardin grey slacks and my Gucci loafers...Before I knew it, off came my double-breasted blazer, my Pierre Cardin grey slacks and my Gucci loafers and I found myself spread-eagled in the nude on a bed.* **[10]**

The first in a trilogy shot in and around Jersey City, this tells of a small town society girl drafted in as an undercover detective to investigate a prostitution and drugs ring, one of whose members raped her when she was sixteen. The lead in all three films is Cheri Caffaro, a lofty blonde who as a teenager had won a Brigitte Bardot lookalike competition, and whose husband Don Schain, scripted and directed the series.

"Every man wants her, No man can tame her!" boasts the tagline, as we see Ginger McAllister driving into town. Henceforth she will use her body to entrap criminals, not always with pleasant results. The story is sexist, *profoundly* racist, and politically incorrect—everyone's favourite word is "bitch". The actors' lines are frequently fluffed, and there is an unattractive quota of hairy female armpits and bad tan-lines while the men, Rodney aside, all have paunches. But, it is never boring.

Rodney is part of the cartel, who one by one are dealt with by the sexually aggressive Ginger. She drugs his drink, and when he comes to he is naked and full-frontal—Casey Donovan in all his hirsute glory, spread-eagled on the bed with his hands and feet bound. Licking her lips and saying how much she is enjoying the view, Ginger toys with a length of piano-wire while giving Rodney a history lesson. During World War Two, she says, Japanese concentration camp guards tortured prisoners by stripping them naked and tying them to stakes in the parade ground, then getting a naked woman to walk among them—the punishment being that those who got erections were castrated. Now, she attaches the wire to Rodney's testicles, and says she wants answers to

19

how he operates. Stripping naked, she lies on top of him and he cannot resist kissing her and of course getting hard. And though she gets her answers, she still tightens the wire and castrates him.

Though the film was still on *Variety*'s list of *Top Box Office Grossing Independent Films* list when it and its sequels were re-released on DVD in 2002, the magazine's critic at the time gave it a thumbs-down adding, "Only Calvin Culver as the thrill-seeking jet set blackmailer shows any indication of better things to come."

Cal's parents flew into to New York for the film's March 1971 premiere, and he remembered:

> *The producer, worried about how my mother would take her son's nudity onscreen, took her aside and said, "Now, Mrs. Culver, there are certain explicit things in this picture, and you must expect to be shocked." She replied, "Shocked? I doubt it. Bored, maybe."* [11]

In the meantime, when shooting wrapped, Cal went back to treading the boards, gaining his Equity card and making his Broadway debut in Joseph Golden's *Brave* at the ANTA Theater. Staged by the Robert Kennedy Theater for Children, this was a musical revue promoting the legacy of the Native Indian— an extravaganza far removed from *Ginger* it opened on 2 April, and despite being denounced by Cal as "a two day abortion" received good reviews and showed great promise, but was forced to close after just six performances on account of a newspaper strike.

20

Days later, Cal was approached by Jerry Douglas, then involved with the off-Broadway theatre scene, and who later become one of the undisputed doyennes of gay porn. Douglas' latest play, *Circle in the Water*, had bombed at the box-office, but rather than close the production down, he elected to fire the entire cast and hire a new one. The director recalled of Cal:

> *He was a perfect archetype, ideal casting for the co-starring role of a popular athlete whose allure brings to the boil the simmering tensions among closeted young cadets at a Michigan military academy. During weeks of wholesale rewrites and restaging, he proved to be an unflappable professional who was never late to rehearsals, was the first to know his lines, and was enormously popular with the cast. There was an easygoing charm and affability about him, but he always vanished promptly after each performance, not to be heard of until his next call. [12]*

In the play, Cal played Lieutenant Gregg Chandler, whose good looks bring about unprecedented sexual attraction and sadism from his fellow cadets at the academy. He recalled:

> *I was bent over a stool and soundly whipped with a belt. The show was a piece of shit but our director, Jerry Douglas, kept rewriting it and each day it got better until it was almost an interesting play....The third to last*

21

performance I was manhandled so much I was very badly bruised and I also cracked a rib. But when I learned that Sylvia Miles and Shelley Winters were in the audience, I decided the show must go on and I ordered them to tape me up. That performance, the audience really got their sadistic kicks because I was in agony from the time the curtain went up till the time it came down again.

Circle in the Water closed prematurely on 28 June 1970—such was the level of homophobia levelled at it that the theatre received two bomb threats. As if distrusting of his increasing fame, Cal did not let success go to his head, and kept on modelling for Wilhelmina and working at Serendipity 3—earning considerably more from discreetly cruising clients than he did from waiting on tables. He also signed short-term contracts with the TMI Agency, run by Dovina (Dorothy Juba, 1927-90), reputed to have been the highest-paid fashion model of her day—and Bill Blass (1922-2002), just starting out on what would be an extremely lucrative solo venture. Blass, a client of Cal's, hired him to model his exclusive range of sportswear.

In July 1970, Cal was approached by a director named Seemore Doules, almost certainly not his real name and probably a client, of whom nothing is known. Doules was about to start shooting *Eleana*, the first in a trilogy of soft-core hour-long features. The tagline was, "An epic of lost innocence…a 'liberated' single girl learns how to set a week-end aflame!" He was billed as J. Calvin Culver, and his co-star was the now forgotten Athena Prezaki. This would be premiered in Chicago in December 1970, and like its successors, *Jennifer* and *Marina*, quickly be assigned to oblivion. There was no chance however of such a fate befalling Calvin Culver, as fame and glory were waiting just around the corner.

Cal Culver, Wilhelmina model.

2: *Casey*

It's fun to be up there on the screen. You can become a fantasy figure for a lot of people. Look at how many people fantasise on Clark Gable and Marilyn Monroe. If people don't fantasise on you as a star, you're not gonna be a star. And a lot of people have gotten off on Casey Donovan. (Casey)

It was through a friend of Seemore Doules—he maintained that this was a woman he had worked with in *Ginger*—that Cal was asked to audition for the part of Casey, in the film of the same name, after the actor penciled in for the part dropped out. He recalled in an interview of 1973:

> *I originally did it for the money...I was desperate and I needed bread. It was a lot of money at the time, $125 a day. That's a lot of bread. A lot of people are lucky to make that in two weeks...I had no money at that time. So I went to see this guy on a Wednesday, and on Saturday we started filming.* [1]

Casey was shot in New Jersey over a 15-day period. Some of the sex is simulated, but this does not deflect from the quality of the production. Cal displays an innate sense of humour, his charisma leaps off the screen and, because he had started out on the stage and knew how to act and pronounce his lines clearly, his performance is considerably more articulate, polished and credible than the majority of the "Suck that dick!" A-list porn stars of his and the next generation.

Four days after signing the contract, Cal reported to the set, having been told not to engage in any kind of sexual activities for two days before the cameras started rolling—the "norm" for porn stars to guarantee a good "money-shot", an instruction which he promptly ignored. Thus while co-stars Nat Grey and Angelo Waine ejaculate, Cal never does. Despite his love of exhibitionism, he claimed that it was a tough film to make. For reasons known only to the director, the crew and the three other actors were straight—though one might argue that once a scene had wrapped, Waine and Grey were no longer technically thus, as they quite obviously enjoy what they are doing. Cal observed:

> *It was kind of a very uptight situation. One kid turned out to be married and very straight. I don't think he'd ever been involved with a guy before, and he was obviously doing it for the money. I thought, "Wow, you know, come on. If you're going to do it, be into doing it, because if you're not you're going to look terrible." But he was cast, so what could I do? There was another guy who was very uptight, and the problem was my having to make them look good.* [2]

Cal also said that he had to "get hard to pay for his supper", but he does not get fully hard in any of his scenes, which is perhaps immaterial. In parts it is an astonishingly romantic production—with its jazz-swing soundtrack almost like French New Wave, but with hard-core sex. It opens with Casey in bed, masturbating under the covers. Even this he finds boring, stopping to switch on the television, pop a pill, and read a magazine before faking his climax. Then he goes into the bathroom, where he sings to himself in front of the mirror—the opening bars of "Everything's Coming Up Roses" before spitting out the word, "Faggot!" A health freak, he scoffs a handful of vitamin pills from the row of bottles here, then takes a slug of bourbon—"Over the teeth, over the gums, I gotta stomach, here it comes!"—and finally lights a joint! Suddenly, he conjures up his fairy godmother, Wanda Uptight—Cal in drag, and playing the part inordinately well in a long black wig, rhinestone headband, and making no effort to cover his hairy chest. He recalled,

> *I looked like Doris Day shot through linoleum, it was just incredible. I really thought it was going to be a piece of real shit, and I thought, "Take the money and run." But when I saw it all put together, I was absolutely amazed what happened to it. It was really pretty good.* **[3]**

Wanda rebukes him for dragging her away from her "pansy-patch", and asks him how his haemorrhoids are, and if he has yet acquired any STDs. When he touches his penis she tells him that excessive masturbation will give him pimples. She asks him what he wants, and he tells her he is bored with his mundane sex life, which amounts to sleeping with a different man every night—that what he *really* wants is a man he will care about, and who will care about him. Before vanishing, Wanda grants him his wish. There is a knock on the door and The Crotch (Sparrow Guano) appears—to prove to the world that he is heterosexual, the actor wears his wedding ring, and in this first scene, only his lower half is seen. He and Casey share a joint, and Casey fellates him—The Crotch does not get an erection, and Casey ends up with a wet facial...of hand-cream!

Next up, we Casey watching Delivery Boy (Angelo Waine) the hunk from the grocery store across the street. He calls, and orders potatoes and beer. Delivery Boy turns up. He is in such good shape, he says, because he chews gum and swims are lot. He adds that potatoes make him horny, and bites into a raw one. He drops the bag, and they strip and roll around the kitchen floor among the spuds in an extended fellatio scenario. Then when they are done Delivery Boy leaves, and The Crotch returns to simulate anal sex with Casey up against the kitchen unit while Casey, desperate to feel needed, asks him beseechingly, "Do you *like* me? If I had no ass...if I was a Martian with a hole in my elbow would you *still* like me?" The Crotch's response before leaving is to tell Casey that he talks too much—in other words, to some gay (and straight) men in these hedonistic times, it is only the sex that matters, and not getting to know who one is having it with.

It is here that romance takes over, in a scene that is beautifully filmed and one of the most memorable of any 1970s gay adult film. Wanda reappears, and tells Casey that his future will amount to little more than a series of tawdry episodes on downtown tearooms, unless he amends his ways. "That's bullshit," he snaps back. "I stopped cruising subways when I was twelve!" He therefore asks her to make him irresistible because he still has not achieved his goal—a man who will want him for himself, and *not* just for the sex. She tells him to go for a walk and pick a flower, and the actor and the part combine as Casey/Cal leaves the house wearing his tweeds, shirt and tie as was happening in real life. Outside, a hunky art student is sitting on the grass, nursing his sketch-pad. This is Stephen (Nat Grey), who follows him into the woods. Giggling like giddy schoolboys, they chase each other around the trees, until Stephen catches Casey and they enter a grassy clearing where he uses his sketch pad for communication because he has taken a vow of silence until the Vietnam War is over. To say that Grey is endearing and possessed of all the right requisites for gay porn may be putting it mildly, and it is a great pity that he never appeared in another adult film. They have sex, and what follows is a glorious summer of love. Casey and Stephen move in together, and Stephen serves him breakfast wearing just a skimpy apron. This time when they have sex, Casey's "money-shot" is hilarious—camera trickery, aided by a hidden squeezy bottle which spurts a vast amount of hand-cream two feet into the air! The scene closes with Stephen sketching Casey, while he eats his breakfast.

Two months pass. Then Casey is back at the window, eyeing the hunks in the street below. Dissatisfied with having sex with just one man, he tells Stephen that they need is a party. Therefore he invites Delivery Boy over, and he and Stephen share him, resulting in the film's only actual penetration scene when Delivery Boy tops Casey, who delivers another hand-cream ejaculation. Even so it is an idyllic moment, until The Crotch reappears and we get to hear him speak and see what he really looks like—a huge black man with a massive Afro hairstyle. He is also some kind of seer, probably sent by Wanda to teach Casey a lesson by telling him that he knows nothing about "tender loving care". He asks the other three to strip him naked, and they lay Casey on the floor, and fondle him while he closes his eyes and mutters to himself in ecstasy. When he opens his eyes, the other three are gone, a reflection of what has happened after his endless succession of one-night stands, and he goes into the bathroom where Wanda reappears to tell him that he has blown his chance of lasting happiness. He begs her to help him, and she tells him that he must get a grip and start all over again. The film ends with him picking up the sketchpad Stephen has left behind, and masturbating while looking at his lover's self-portrait.

Cal was a fan of the British singer Donovan, and while shooting *Casey* told director Donald Crane that he wanted to be billed not as Calvin Culver but as Ken Donovan, so that his family would not find out that he was making porn. Then after considering that he had so much in common with his on-screen character, he changed his mind again:

> *One day I heard a Donovan song on the radio. Casey Donovan, I thought. That's kind of neat. I wanted another name—to use*

29

for these hardcore jobs—because I was modelling by then, and of course there was my family to consider. My parents have a family-owned motel and my brother, who's in his thirties, is not in show business. [4]

For now, the new name only applied to this film, as Cal had solved his financial problems and was not interested in appearing in another hard-core production. Returning to New York, he resumed his modeling career, and went back to waiting on tables and discreetly hustling interested parties at Serendipity 3.

It was courtesy of the restaurant's co-proprietor, Calvin Holt, that Cal's next project came about. While *Casey* was being edited, Cal and his lover Donald headed for Fire Island, where they rented a house in Cherry Grove for two weeks. Holt and his friend, sexploitation director Andy Milligan, were about to start shooting a comedy-drama film here, *Dragula*, a spin-off of *Dracula* of which virtually nothing is known other than it was a gay soft-core vampire movie in which Dracula's sons—one good and over-the-top camp, the other narcissistic, evil and power-mad—are pitted against each other. Holt, who edited a gay magazine, financed the project by hiring just one on the twelve writers in his pool to write an entire issue—and used the other eleven salaries as collateral to back the film.

When one reflects on Casey Donovan's career, *Dragula* is regarded as insignificant—hardly any of his fans have seen it, and indeed prints of the film may no longer exist. What *is* important is that it, and the location where it was shot, led to him being cast for the production which brought him world fame. At this point in his career, he nurtured no intention of appearing in another hardcore porn movie, and when a mutual friend gave him the contact details of a porn director eager to work with him, he merely promised he would *think* about it.

Before *Casey*, there had been few half-decent gay porno flics, certainly of a non-sleazy nature. Loops, as they were called, were shot in seedy locations on tiny budgets. Romance, affection and comedy were unheard of traits. Gay men were rarely perceived as having feelings, but "fuck-and-forget" stereotypes. If they were hirsute and leather-clad, so much the better for the producers, while those compelled to watch them, because there was no alternative, were given the very wrong impression that *their* own kind of closeted homosexuality was extant of the norm—that sex, aggression and tawdry conditions were essential requirements for the gay man who wanted to have fun with other gay men.

Enter Wakefield Poole, the pioneering director who—with Casey Donovan, the name with which he will be henceforth referred to here—brought class, romance, and above all *normality* to gay pornography.

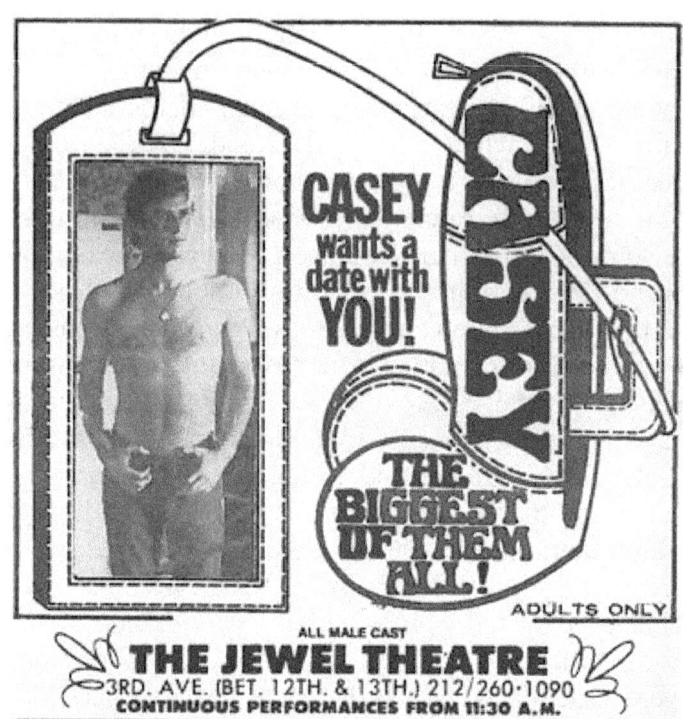

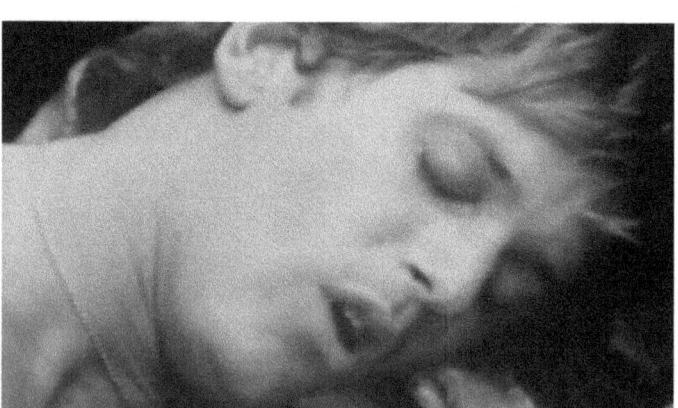

Casey (1971), the film which provided Cal Culver
with his famous pseudonym.

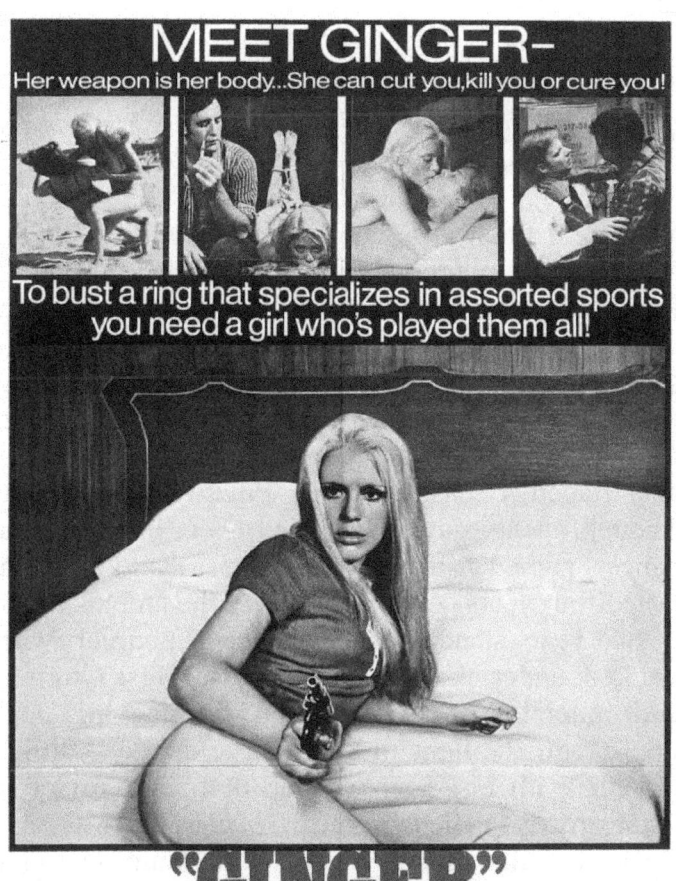

The name Calvin Culver did not appear on the
playbill of *Ginger* (1971), but today the film is
remembered only for Casey's participation.

3: *Boys in the Sand*

I'm very proud of Boys, because I think it's a very beautiful film and one of the best of its kind that's ever been made. It's kind of a classic. (Casey)

Wakefield Poole was born in Jacksonville, Florida, around 1936. A trained dancer, he joined the Ballet Russe de Monte Carlo in 1957, and later became a choreographer-director on Broadway working in such productions as *West Side Story* and *The Unsinkable Molly Brown*—and on television in *The Gerry Moore Show* and *The Ed Sullivan Show*. He also staged a season of *The Phyllis Diller Show*. Though openly gay, he married once, in 1964 to a dancer named Nancy Van Rijn, a union which lasted four years. After his divorce, he and his lover of two years standing, Peter Schneckenburger (who worked under the pseudonym Peter Fisk) turned their attention to experimental film-making, and Poole "saw the light" after going to the Park-Miller Theatre with Fisk and a group of friends to see a "monstrosity" called *Highway Hustler*.

Shot on film in four loops, with Danny Det and Dick Fuller, *Highway Hustler* tells of a hitch-hiker who is abducted and sodomized at gunpoint—to a soundtrack of "June Is Busting Out All Over". Poole recalled that after watching it, he felt like he had done something his mother had told him not to do—how Fisk found the film so depressing that he fell asleep, and that this inspired him to make a film that gay people could identify with.

34

Fisk had recently bought Poole a movie camera, and for the past few weeks they had been experimenting with this and now felt it that it was time to put it to good use. The result was a ten-minute short shot on Fire Island, a favourite weekend retreat of Poole and Fisk. Partnering Fisk was an Italianate man named Dino, who worked in a local gift shop.

The sequence told of a chance gay encounter in the Meat Rack, one of the island's main cruising areas, which Poole entitled *Bayside*. He showed it to friends, and such was their enthusiasm that they suggested he shoot two more segments, enough for a full-length feature, and seek backing for theatrical distribution. Poole teamed up with a producer friend named Marvin Shulman, and they formed Poolemar Productions. There were problems when Dino heard about the possible production deal and demanded $2,000 for his participation, along with 20% of any profits. Poole was having none of this, and when a mutual friend, Joe Nelson, introduced him to Casey, history was in the making. Poole recalled:

> *When I opened the door the first thing I saw was this incredible smile on a very handsome face. His look was perfect—the type you see in magazine ads, not porno movies. I showed him the section with Peter and Dino. When it was over, Cal stood up and said, "I want to do it! You just tell me what to do and I'll do it. It's really great. When do we start?* [1]

Poole later observed how he *only* needed to see a face to work out if an actor was screen-perfect:

35

Actually, even though I want my actors to make love to the camera, I very seldom have them strip. Sometimes I do when in doubt. I mean, in an audition, with three of us interviewing the prospect we might say, "Drop your jeans and get it hard." That's more for the shock therapy than for any exploitation. I cast basically by feedback, aura, securities, insecurities. I find faces as important, if not more important, to my films than genitalia. That's the essence of cinema: face. Not tits or ass or cock or fist. Face. [2]

Casey was *so* impressed that he offered to work for Poole for nothing! He *was* paid $500, the amount he had been paid for *Casey*, along with the promise of a handsome bonus for each $12,000 the film took at the box-office—providing that it got this far and proved successful. The sequence with Peter Fisk and Dino was re-shot with Fisk and Casey, and the result was so perfect that Poole decided to film two more segments, *Poolside* and *Inside* and, as had happened with *Casey*, reconstruct a storyline around him. Filming took place on Fire Island, over three weekends in August 1981, on a budget of $8,000.

For *Poolside*, Poole hired 32-year-old Danny DiCiccio, a local handyman who had also appeared in Colt loops as The Carpenter, in reference to his trade. Casey said he had been trying to get him into bed for some time, and now he had a legitimate reason for poaching him away from his lover, if but for a little while. For *Inside*, Casey recommended an African-American former trick named Tommy Moore, who worked as a barman on Fire Island.

Bayside opens to a Debussy soundtrack, and with the title and the name "Casey Donovan" etched into the sand. Then we see bearded Peter Fisk heading for the beach, where he spreads out his sheet, strips naked, and reclines to gaze out across the horizon. In the distance, Casey materializes from the water and runs towards the sand, in slow motion, his impressive appendage swaying from side to side. There is no dialogue, and henceforth everything is improvised, the sex natural and unscripted. Casey wears a cock-ring, Fisk a cock-strap. He stands before Fisk, who places the flat of his hand on his stomach, then proceeds to fellate him. For the first time—this never happened in *Casey*—we see Casey with a full erection—a thick, eight-inch, attractive circumcised penis, but with more skin than most cut American porn stars, and which remains hard throughout the production, even in non-sexual scenes. After a little while, Casey indicates for Fisk to follow him into the bushes. The sun flickers through the leaves and across Casey's profile as he gazes skyward, making him appear almost angelic. Removing the studded leather strap from Fisk's wrist, he fastens this around his penis and testicles, and they take turns penetrating each other, resulting in Casey's very first *genuine* on-screen money-shot. The scene could easily be one of voyeurism, with cameraman Poole hiding out of sight, and the two men blithely unaware that they are being watched and filmed. When they are done, Fisk removes his cock-strap and fastens it about Cal's wrist before running into the sea and disappearing, while Casey dresses in Fisk's abandoned clothes, assumes his identity, and returns to the boardwalk. **[3]**

In *Poolside,* Casey is sitting on a wall with a copy of *Gay Magazine* tucked under his arm. He heads for the "Frank House", which itself was a kind of celebrity, owned by friends of his, and which fits in well with Poole's avant-garde approach to film-making. Designed by the architect Andrew Geller, it had been built in 1958 for ice-cream entrepreneur Rudy Frank, who had visited the Mayan ruins at Uxmal, in Mexico, and been so inspired by the many-stepped Pyramid of the Magician that he had asked Geller to come up with something along these lines, with inward-sloping walls. The house stood on a high sand-hill overlooking the Atlantic Ocean, and had wide decks on three sides, a catwalk crossing the living area, and an all-glass façade. There was also a door high up on one side—which opened on to a long drop to the grounds below. Introducing the viewer to the property, Casey is greeted by the owner's shaggy dog, who naturally recognizes him. He goes to the pool, strips and gets on to a sun-lounger, where he reads the paper. The "Wanton Ads" column is on the back page, and in the pool-house he pens a letter in response to one of these, signing it with his own name before returning to the boardwalk where he mails this. We see him jogging along the beach, then disappearing calendar pages signify the passing of time. Some of these float on the pool where Casey affects what he called his "Esther Williams swimming routine". Next, he walks to the post-office to collect his reply, which arrives in the form of a package. Returning to the pool, he strips naked, gets hard as if aware of what is about to happen, and opens this. It contains a large, alka-seltzer type pill which he throws into the pool. This churns, and the phenomenally-endowed Danny DiCiccio materializes out of the water. He is a hirsute hulk of a man with whom Casey engages in acrobatic but rough turn-and-turn-about sex on the decking, their complicated positions among the flickering shadows choreographed by Wakefield Poole, but still looking perfectly natural. The Colt loops that Danny had appeared in contained erections, but only simulated sex, made to look real by way of clever camera angles. This may explain that while Casey climaxes, he does not. They then roll into the pool, and after a little gentle horseplay towel each other dry and go down to the beach— sitting on the wall is Ed Parente, a friend of Wakefield Poole engaged for the stills photography, and who is reading the same newspaper that Casey was reading earlier. Parente walks off, in the hope of history repeating itself.

Inside opens, giving the viewer no clue as to what has happened to Danny. Casey is naked and spread-eagled face-down on the bed as the morning sun filters through the window. He gets up, gets hard, showers, towels himself dry, and crosses to the window where he sees Tommy Moore walking past, checking the poles. Casey begins masturbating and watches him, first through the net curtain, then in full view on the balcony, but Moore does not seem interested. At this point, Casey walks around the house, fantasizing. The camera cuts away between scenes, incorporating flashing images of the wall panels to separate them. Casey sees Tommy on a downstairs bunk, naked but for his work-belt. They start having sex, until our hero briefly returns to reality to sniff poppers and sodomize himself with a

39

large black dildo, a replica of Tommy's penis. The fantasy resumes with a naked Tommy lying face down on the bed. They kiss, fellate and top each other until Casey returns to the dildo, and climaxes. Then the fantasy ends and we see Casey where this began, drying himself after his shower. Finally, Moore knocks on the door and Casey invites him in, one would hope so that they can do for real what he has just imagined. What made the scene different, at the time, was that it was one of the first interracial gay scenes to appear on celluloid. Casey recalled:

> *I was freshest when I did that one, People have since told me, "But he's so black!" I wouldn't have cared if he was green. I dug him, and that was all that mattered.* [4]

Shooting wrapped, with none of the participants—Wakefield Poole included—knowing what would happen next. Casey returned to waiting on tables at Serendipity 3, hustling, and doing fashion shoots for Wilhelmina. Another of their leading lights, the German fashion model Uva Harden, was halfway through shooting *Some of My Best Friends Are*, a musical melodrama directed by Mervyn Nelson. Appearing with him was Andy Warhol musc Candy Darling, and future *Golden Girl* Rue McClanahan. Harden introduced Casey to Nelson, and he was given a small part in the film—that of a self-loathing hustler. He was listed as Calvin Culver on the call-sheet, though his name was left off the credits. It was not a good film but it did show that since the 1969 Stonewall riots, little had changed on the New York gay scene where prejudice and attitudes were concerned. The action takes place on Christmas Eve in Greenwich Village, in an establishment referred to by one client as "a pansy-perch, a haven for homosexuals". It is a sad story. Even so it remains watchable as a curiosity. Writing in *The New York Times* after the premiere at the Twin Theaters, Vincent Canby observed:

> In almost every way, it's a second-rate spin-off from *The Boys in the Band*. Yet because of this second-rateness, which includes hammy performances and a sentimental screenplay that sounds as if it had just been let out after thirty years in a closet, it may well be more accurate than the slicker, wittier *Boys in the Band*. When most of the characters in a movie are as full of dopey sentiments, as well as of self-hatred and of self-exploitation as the movie that contains them, it's almost impossible to differentiate between an intentional second-rateness and serious moviemaking of no great quality. It's impossible, that is, until it becomes obvious that Mervyn Nelson shares with his characters not only a large amount of boozy self-pity, but also the sort of romanticism that permits characters to define themselves without irony, in the clichés of old-fashioned Hollywood soap operas. [5]

The film delivers every stereotype, prejudice and over-the-top cliché. The characters are presented as unhappy, neurotic, hysterical—and unable to sustain

41

relationships, and with no life to speak of extant of the Blue Jay Bar. As resident "fag-hag" Lita Joyce, Rue McClanahan is not sure if she is imitating Tallulah Bankhead or Bette Davis, and throws in a little of Marlene Dietrich's "Boys in the Backroom" for good measure. Uva Harden, speaking to his older closeted lover about the risks he takes as a ski instructor, opines, "Facing death does not take courage. Two men facing a life together does." There is a closeted priest, and two intensely disturbing scenarios. The first is when the man who has been chatting up Karen (Candy Darling), gropes her, discovers that she is transgender, and subsequently beats her to a pulp. The second is when a mother, who has followed her son and seen him enter a gay bar, confronts him and screams, "Why didn't you tell me you were sick? I'd have got a doctor."

Boys in the Band similarly influenced Wakefield Poole's choice of a title for his film. He chose *Boys in the Sand*, and rented New York's 200-seater 55th Street Playhouse, where Andy Warhol had exhibited his *Lonesome Cowboys* two years earlier. Since then the interior had fallen into a state of disrepair, and ahead of the 29 December 1971 premiere a team of cleaners and decorators worked around the clock to bring the place up to scratch. Such an opening for a porn film was unheard of in those days, and came in the wake of Poole's brave publicity campaign which had seen him organizing screen parties attended by such luminaries as Leonard Bernstein and Casey's idol, Steven Sondheim, and placing ads in *Variety* and *The New York Times*—the first gay display ad the newspaper had ever accepted. Pool recalled:

To this day, I don't know how we got such placement. The ad looked classy, so maybe they didn't read the copy. Or perhaps someone had let it slip by. I'd like to think some gay man in the advertising department had pulled some strings. If that is what happened, I'm forever grateful. [6]

The ad, which appeared on the same page as the ones promoting Elizabeth Taylor's film *X, Y and Zee* and *Nicholas and Alexandra*, featured a playbill designed by Ed Parente—Wakefield Poole's stills photographer, and the man seen sitting on the fence in *Poolside*. This had been designed before Casey had replaced Dino—the man in it does not resemble him one bit. Sporting a 1920s-style moustache, he wears a Speedo, across the crotch of which is a lightning bolt. Around his shoulder is a sash of seashells, while around his right bicep and wrist are leather thongs. Clutched against his thigh is a beach ball. The whole is encased in an Art Deco frame, and would be subsequently replaced by one which featured Casey.

Boys in the Sand's reception was unprecedented. Pre-dating *Deep Throat* by six months, it was the first porn film to achieve crossover success into the mainstream. Poole and his producer-partner Marvin Shulman were also aware of the risks involved with screening a gay porn film with such a fanfare of advance publicity, at a time when these were still illegal in America, and invariably shown at sleazy downtown cinemas far-removed from the cleaned up Playhouse, usually with someone standing guard at the door on the lookout for the police.

43

The fact that there was no dialogue worked in the film's favour. Like some of the great silent stars—one instinctively thinks of Rudolph Valentino—Casey Donovan was capable of saying more with an expression than some might put into words. Each man watching him could easily believe that these expressions, never lewd, were directed at him alone. *Boys in the Sand* recovered its production costs by close of business on the day that it opened, and four times this amount during its first week. It played to packed audiences in New York for nineteen weeks. During its first six months, as Casey's fame spread countrywide and then across the globe, it grossed over $200,000.

The reviews too were unprecedented for this genre of film, many critics comparing Wakefield Poole to Andy Warhol, Kenneth Anger and some of the European avant-garde directors. *The Advocate* observed of porn's newest superstar, "Everyone will fall in love with this philandering fellator." *Gay Insider* enthused, "It is impossible to ignore Casey's magnificence, or to minimize his impact. I adore him!" And from *Village Voice*, "Casey Donovan looks like a liberated Robert Redford. He is mated with men who are exotic contrasts to him."

Films & Filming's Peter Buckley reminded his readers that a good many straight couples and single women were flocking to see the film, and observed for those yet to see it:

> *All four 'boys' are men, each one representing a differing type: the all-American blond collegiate surfer, the sensitive thinker, the muscle man and the big*

sensuous black...Every cinematic technique in the book seems to have been successfully utilized at one time or another, and it's almost as if Bo Widerberg and Ken Russell got together to make an honest hardcore homo flick.

Gay Sunshine was more to the point:

Casey Donovan is a trim, golden-blond Apollo, a pleasure to behold. He has an idealized classic, awe-inspiring physique, without the slightest trace of faggotry or gayness, guaranteeing the film's success, whatever its flaws....poor lighting and over-exposure (no pun) in exterior scenes, a casual uninflected editing scheme, and rather carelessly done camera effects. These however can be seen as minor irritations. After all, Poole's film didn't have to achieve much here to prove superior to its predecessors.

Some of these "flaws" were highlighted by Aaron Bates of *Gay Magazine*, the publication given a plug in the film's middle section, though the critic's general observations were enthusiastic:

There is ample food here for one's daydreams, as well as for one's night dreams. It gives the audience exactly what is needed, plus a little more....Some of the photography left much to be desired. Although generally consistent, certain small

45

scenes were underexposed, overexposed, or lacking focus. Certain footage should have been scissored. I found the musical scoring rather offensive, particularly in the first episode in which a choir of soprano banshees appear to be keening in the background while the lovers hump their way to happiness. This might be considered an improvement over the typical muzak found in this type of movie, but I wonder. On the other hand...it gives the audience exactly what is needed—fresh and well-hung meat, plus a little more for the price of admission.

After its first week, the film reached Number 46 on *Variety*'s Top Box Office 50 list, ahead of *X, Y and Zee*, and taking more money at the box-office than the Elizabeth Taylor film. "Robe", their critic, proclaimed, "There are no more closets!" He added:

It's so *cinema-verité* that at times the viewer fears the camera itself is going to get into the action. As the action in a series of repetitive movements, the only variation the film offers is in a series of assorted backgrounds. The casting, which appears to have been done by Dial-A-Hustler, seems to have had one requirement, that the applicant be anatomically equipped for some strenuous exercise. The film has been booked for the 55th St. Playhouse on a four-wall deal. Where it goes after that depends on how much interest the Morality in Media people display in it.

Gay Magazine, in its next issue and this time with the reviewer choosing to remain anonymous, proffered praise—and a somewhat back-handed compliment: "There is ample food here for one's daydreams, as well as for one's night dreams. It gives the audience exactly what is needed, plus a little more."

Michael's Thing, at the time an essential weekly guide to porn theatres, shows, baths and other gay recreational activities in New York and New Jersey, enthused:

> To a connoisseur of the cinema, it is the most decadent of sexploitation skin flics, and to a dirty old man it is the ultimate art film. Whether you are a lecher or a gymnast, *Boys in the Sand* has something to teach you! [7]

Wakefield Poole told Jack Fritscher:

> *That atmosphere* [of the film] *was very controlled. That's why straight film reviewers took notice.* Boys in the Sand *was the first gay film that straights perceived as not sleazy...So many people say, "God, you changed my life! I saw Casey Donovan sit on a dildo in Boys in the Sand. I heard men did that, but when I saw a beautiful man plug himself, suddenly that became all right for me. So I went out and bought one!"* [8]

Virtually overnight, Casey Donovan became *the* underground sensation in New York, while his fame travelled rapidly across America. Few cities in the country screened gay porn, but the film did big business in San Francisco, Washington, Boston, Portland, Houston, Dallas, Minneapolis, Seattle, Denver, Chicago and Philadelphia. Every closeted gay celebrity wanted Casey at their parties and receptions.

On 9 February 1972, the film opened at Los Angeles' 1100-seater Paris Theatre, where one of the special guests was Rock Hudson. After the screening, Rock invited Casey to a party at his home, the Castle, the next evening and one thing led to another. Off and on over the next ten years, the pair would meet up whenever they could. Rock had a penchant *only* for muscular blonds, and Casey fit the bill perfectly.

Another valued "connection" at around this time was Alan Helms, who later penned *Young Man from the Provinces: A Gay Life Before Stonewall*, a feted memoir of his days as an ethereal-looking "golden boy star-fucker" of the sophisticated gay worlds of Europe and America. Amongst his conquests were Anthony Perkins, Leonard Bernstein and Luchino Visconti. Thirty-four when he had encountered Casey on the beach—he claimed by chance—Helms would see him, off and on for several years:

> *When we met, I fortunately hadn't yet seen him in* Boys in the Sand. *If I had, I might have been disabled when Cal-Casey walked out of the Fire Island surf in a Speedo, made a beeline to me, and we retired to my place just off the boardwalk. But then I saw his movie, and thereafter whenever we had sex,*

48

I felt like one of his partners in Boys in the Sand*...suddenly trapped in someone else's pornographic fantasy, maneuvered and constrained by another's desires, and the feeling soon ruined the sex for me. Nevertheless, since Cal-Casey desired me and most of gay America desired him, I figured that I mattered a lot, and my life thus had meaning.* **[9]**

Thirteen years on, when Casey and Wakefield Poole were shooting the sequel, *Boys in the Sand II*, on Fire Island, Robert Richards observed in *Stallion*:

Viewed today by current standards, *Boys* may seem tame and dated. But if it weren't for this trailblazer, would our current standards be where they are? *Birth of a Nation* is dated by today's standards, yet its innovations set film-making on a course for growth. Likewise *Boys* was innovative in ways that shaped today's standards, and its influence continues to be felt. **[10]**

49

10th SMASH WEEK

"THERE ARE NO MORE CLOSETS." —Variety, 1/19/72

12:20; 1:45; 3:10; 4:35; 6:00; 7:25; 8:50; 10:15.

Fire Island . . . Uncensored
WAKEFIELD POOLE'S

BOYS IN THE SAND

ALL MALE CAST   IN COLOR   FOR MATURE ADULTS

A POOLEMAR PRODUCTION   STARRING CASEY DONOVAN

IN NEW YORK CITY:	IN LOS ANGELES:
55TH STREET PLAYHOUSE	**PARIS THEATER**
(BET. 6th & 7th AVES.)	8163 Santa Monica Blvd.
JU 6-4590	469-9475

The original Ed Parente poster for *Boys in the Sand*
(1971) before Casey replaced Dino.

50

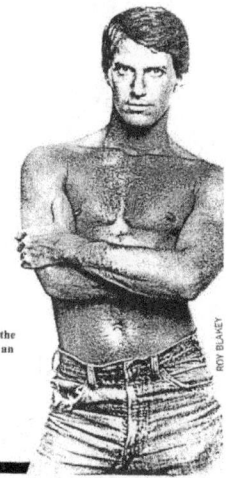

THE MOST ACCLAIMED
MALE MOVIE IN THE
HISTORY OF CINEMA

WAKEFIELD POOLE'S

BOYS IN THE SAND

STARRING CASEY DONOVAN

"A great leap forward...Poole managed to keep the right balance...(it's) as if Ken Russell had made an honest homo flick."—FILMS AND FILMING.

ROY BLAKEY

The subsequent poster, with Casey.

In the Meat Rack, Casey anticipates....

Poolside: Casey and Danny DiCoccio lock lips…

….and afterwards head for the boardwalk.

4: *The Back Row*

Casey Donovan was a delight—personally, professionally, sexually. You name it, he had it all going for him. (Wakefield Poole)

Casey did not allow success to go to his head, aware that *Boys in the Sand* might be a flash in the pan. To this aim, he continued working at Serendipity B, and still put his modelling work before all else. In February 1972, he responded to an ad in *Variety*. Stephen Porter was putting on a revival of George Bernard Shaw's *Captain Brasshound's Conversion*, at the Ethel Barrymore Theater.

Set in Morocco at the turn of the century, this had first been staged in New York in 1907. The 1960 film version had starred Greer Garson and Christopher Plummer. Porter had cast *Bonanza* star Pernell Roberts in the title role. Ingrid Bergman—who had scored a success in the London production at the Cambridge Theatre the previous spring—would be reprising the part of the explorer, Lady Cicely Waynfleet. The director was now casting the smaller parts and walk-ons, and he and Casey had a history, having enjoyed several one-night stands. Casey auditioned for the part of "American Armed Guard", and when successful told Porter that he wanted to be billed as Calvin Culver. He also was given two uncredited walk-ons, including that of a sailor. Whether Bergman made the link between the two names is not known, but likely—his picture was in several magazines at the time. He recalled:

Ingrid is the loveliest lady in the world. She's absolutely unpretentious. She was supposed to travel first class, but she went everywhere with us, on our terms. She sat in the coach section of the plane, rode on the bus, and took the train just like we all did. She was part of our group. [1]

The play was scheduled to open on Broadway on 17 April. In the meantime, Casey spent his days in the rehearsal studio, and at night flung himself into his latest film project. Though *Boys in the Sand* was still doing big business all over America, more porn roles had not been forthcoming. Many of the big name directors were of the opinion that Wakefield Poole's film had been a fluke—beginner's luck— and refused to change their opinion that burly types such as Dino represented the typical all-American gay male. So-called "swimmer" types such as Casey were considered too effete for the audiences of their crudely cobbled together loops, while Casey himself was not sure that porn was the direction he needed to be travelling in.

It was at this point that Jerry Douglas re-entered his life, having opted to move away from the theatre and shoot his first film. Under the pseudonym Doug Richards, in case this was a failure, he was putting together a project for Hand-in-Hand productions— but one with a difference, that of a clean-cut but worldly city boy who, unlike the one who got his sexual kicks in exotic locations like Fire Island, likes to cruise for sex in dirty toilets, subways, sex-shops and dusty theatres. As part of the deal, Casey would receive a percentage of the profits.

The Back Row may be regarded as the companion-piece to Douglas' *More of a Man* (1991), which sees a guilt-ridden Joey Stefano clutching a rosary and praying to be turned straight—before heading off for the nearest rest-room glory hole. Douglas had seen *Boys in the Sand* at the 55th Street Theater, and remembering how filthy this had been before Poole's cleaners moved in, he decided that his film would be shot in an even seedier environment—the 42nd Street Theater, which at the time screened only porn films. Like Poole he opted for no dialogue, preferring to allow the songs and background music to highlight the physical and mental state of the characters. There was a discussion at the time as to who the singer actually was—William Cox, who composed the neo-New Wave score with vocalese accompaniment, or Casey himself. The voice is certainly similar to his, when one compares it to his brief snatch of singing in *Casey*.

Casey was paid $17,000 for his participation—a staggering amount for an adult star at the time—and much of the film was financed by a man Douglas referred to only as "Big Max". "He looked like a refugee from the road company of *Guys and Dolls*," he recalled. "There was little doubt in my mind that he was a gangster." He also remembered Big Max asking if he and his girlfriend could sit in while it was being shot, bearing in mind that he was putting up the collateral. Douglas put him off by telling him that, to make the actors feel at ease, everyone else involved with the production would be naked—including the cameraman and himself! [2]

Casey's leading man—his obsession throughout the film—was George Payne, a muscular, ethereally handsome, 27-year-old former swimsuit model who had recently arrived in New York. Casey recalled of him, "That boy in the cowboy hat was married and didn't know what side of the fence he was on. He was also difficult to work with."

According to Jerry Douglas, however, Casey was said to have "spotted" Payne in a bar, tested him out by having sex with him, and urged the director to hire him. Unknown at the time, Payne would make a number of classic gay films—the most eclectic being the big-budget *Centurions of Rome* in 1981—before transitioning to straight porn and achieving notoriety for his portrayal of sexual psychopaths, before retiring from the industry in 1988. Douglas is on record as saying that he found him attractive only when he was wearing his character's cowboy hat—and when naked. That Payne was attracted to Casey goes without saying:

> Cal, to me, is beautiful. Just the way he looks. There aren't too many Casey Donovans around. There just aren't people put together like him. Casey's Number One. He's just a turn-on, period. I can't put it in any other words. He's beautiful. Everyone else in the picture was very nice, but like I said, Casey—there's no comparison. [3]

The film opens with a bustling New York scenario of sex-shops and cinema billboards, and a denim-clad Casey, gazing up at one of these before the camera zooms in on his shapely rear. The singer opines, "Your life is like a movie that you're watching from the back row. If you thought that you could change it, would you try?" After deliberating what to do, Casey enters the Park-Miller Cinema and sits on the back row, while the uniformed Sailor and the moustached Hippy (David Knox and Robin Anderson) play footsie, sniff poppers, and have oral sex in the kind of environment where, at the time, it was not unusual for complete strangers to engage in sexual acts while watching the film and then move on to the next adventure—as happens here, after Hippy has ejaculated over Sailor's shoes. He then offers the poppers to Casey, who is not interested, and leaves looking more than a little despondent.

Jerry Douglas shot this sequence as an homage to Alfred Hitchcock, replicating the opening scene of *Strangers on a Train*, where two strangers meet and we see just their feet. The theatre where it was shot screened only heterosexual films, and no effort was made to move the cinemagoers seen sitting behind Knox and Anderson. Unaware that a porn film was being shot, these had walked in and they sit there as if oblivious to what is going on.

Out in the street, Casey's mood changes as he leaps over a barrier and dashes across the square, sending a flock of pigeons soaring skyward. He heads for the Port Authority Bus Station and here, standing on the balcony, he spots the Montana Kid (George Payne) among the crowd—Payne looking butch and drop-dead gorgeous in his sheepskin coat and cowboy hat. The singer croons, "Little boy, little boy won't you come and play with me?" as their eyes meet, and their cat-and-mouse adventure begins. The Kid follows Casey on to the subway, where they sit opposite each other and *almost* play footsie, while each plays mind-games with the other by toying with his crotch—a sequence shot at five in the morning. Casey gets off at Christopher Street and with the Kid hot on his heels heads for the Pleasure Chest. Founded in 1971 by Casey's friend, Duane Colglazier, who appears in the scene in a non-sexual role, this later featured in an episode of *Sex and the City*, and the video of Queen's, "Let Me Entertain You". Here there is a water-bed, which Casey tries out, while there are fantasy flashes alternating between him being fully-clothed and naked, explaining what is happening in the Kid's imagination. When Casey goes into the backroom to look at the various items of bondage gear, the Kid enters the shop and daydreams about him using these—even a dildo and penis-pump. Then he flops on to the water-bed and we witness the ultimate reverie: the Kid naked and spread-eagled on the bed while Casey towers above him, in harness and cap, both of them masturbating. The Kid does not climax, but Casey does, rewarding his protagonist with a copious wet facial while the Kid gazes up at him in ecstasy. [4]

The fantasy over, Casey and the Kid squeeze past each other in the narrow doorway, grinding their crotches together in the confined space, yet still nothing happens. Casey leaves the shop, and the Kid purchases a cock-ring before rushing after him. But while Casey hails a cab, the Kid is short of funds and hitches a ride as the singer opines, "If I could, I would love you forever." Next we see them entering the 42nd Street Cinema. Jerry Douglas recalled that the toilets here were so disgusting that he had to rent two urinals, and install them in the little-used Ladies' Room. Casey buys his ticket first, and Cashier (Warren Carlton) tempts him with his erect penis. Casey is not interested and neither is the Kid, so Cashier returns to his desk and masturbates while the camera zooms in on his pierced frenum. On the screen is a loop, *Roommate Wanted*, with student Arthur Grisham and prospective flat mate Robert Tristan—who Grisham has sex with, to help him decide if he wants to take him in. The fantasy resumes with Casey and the Kid sitting on either side of the aisle, but moving closer to each other as they share a joint. Letting his imagination run wild, the Kid fantasizes that he and Casey are in the scene, with the camera making quick-cuts between the two couples, while the Kid squirms in his seat and gets all hot and bothered.

This film within a film was shot at the apartment of one of Douglas' friends. In the original scenario the actors were to have sex on a glass-topped coffee table, but when Casey and Payne attempted this, the table shattered and they were lucky not to be hurt. Douglas recalled how Casey had laughed off the situation, saying with reference to the scene in *Ginger*, "I don't mind getting a few cuts, but I don't want to be castrated again!" Douglas also claimed that Payne was not penetrated by Casey, but the close-ups in the sequence dictate otherwise.

When the loop ends and the Kid returns to reality, he observes Casey getting it together with Hard Hat (Chris Villette, a New York attorney!) who has just entered the cinema. When they are done, he feels bad about himself, and descends to the men's room to wash his penis in the sink. The Kid does likewise. They make eye-contact, put on cock-rings, and get hard while the singer opines, "Standing too afraid to touch, trembling, wanting you too much." In the days of *agents-provocateurs*, when an anonymous sex partner could have been a plain-clothes police officer, the pair are apprehensive, each waiting for the other to make the first move. Casey, aka Calvin Culver the stage actor, conveys this tense moment well. Then, just as it looks like they are going to get intimate, Hard Hat appears and the Kid makes a hasty exit. An all-out orgy ensues when Casey and Hard Hat have sex, and Cashier joins them as their "bitch". They rip his clothes to shreds, and Casey digs into his bag for his harness, dildo—and candles whose hot wax he drips on to Cashier's chest. Outside, the Kid anxiously paces back and forth. Casey climaxes, and as such is no longer interested in the other two as he dresses and leaves—his rueful expression telling us that he has had enough of these casual encounters and needs to find real love. He approaches the Kid, who is understandably angry and wants nothing to do with him. Finally, he catches up with him in the street and after the briefest dispute the two make up under a sign which says, "Jesus Saves". Happy and smiling, we see them holding hands as they sit facing the river, and Casey knocking off the Kid's hat and getting him to laugh. Finally they enter a telephone booth where they kiss passionately. Casey, however, finds it hard to change his ways and while they are in a tight embrace glances over the Kid's shoulder to make eyes at a bearded hunk who passes by, then pauses to cruise him.

The film was a hit with the box-office, and Jerry Douglas later observed why its successors proved equally successful:

One of the reasons I had whatever success I had in the adult film industry was because I only made one film a year. I had a very good job in New York that I was making a lot of money at, and I had a very wonderful relationship that made me very happy. So on my vacation every year from the magazine [he edited Manshots] *I went to California and made a fuck movie...which nobody else seemed to know how to do. Eight of them won Best Picture. That's a good track record. Eight won Best Actor, eight won Best Director, and seven won Best Screenplay. The adult film industry was very, very good to me. And I was good to it.*
[5]

In 2001, as a tribute to the genius of Jerry Douglas —eleven years after he played Joey Stefano's drag queen mentor in *More of a Man*—director Chi Chi LaRue remade *The Back Row*. Inasmuch as one instinctively knows that it would be an unmitigated disaster remaking *The Sound of Music or Gone With the Wind*, LaRue was taking an uncalculated risk. It was one which paid off, for it is an exceptional film. The replications of the original settings, as much as these could be effected considering the locations had greatly changed over the past thirty years, are tantamount to LaRue's own particular genius. Every movement, nuance and gesture seen in the original production is faithfully reproduced. Canadian stud Ryan Zane is *so* amazing as the Montana Kid that one laments the fact that he made but a handful of films in less than a year before exiting the adult film

61

industry. Kyle Kennedy *does* look out of place much of the time. This is partly because of the considerable difference in height between him and Zane, but mostly on account of his lack of warmth and apprehensive cruising expression, especially in the penultimate men's room scene. Casey Donovan was so possessed of an innate charisma, sincerity and innocent charm, even as a sex-pig as happens here, that he would have proved a tough act for any man to follow. Extant of the sex-scenes, within which he is excellent, Kyle Kennedy fails in every way in his attempts to walk in his shoes.

Yet no sooner had shooting wrapped on *The Back Row* than Casey began worrying that making it had been a big mistake. *Boys In The Sand* had offered romance, displaying to the average closeted gay man that outdoor sex *could* take place in exquisite holiday locations, and not be restricted to iffy cruising areas of public parks. And now here he was, visiting sex shops and wearing items that most men had never seen—and rutting in a threesome on the floor of a dirty toilet! Jerry Douglas recalled:

> *He was worried that Casey's fans might not buy the Golden Boy as a sleaze pig. He was quick to tell me that he had loved doing the scene—had in fact contributed many of the trashiest touches to it—but he was very concerned about how it would affect audiences who had originally seen Casey Donovan in such a different context. He did, he reminded, me, have Casey's reputation to think about.* **[6]**

Casey himself denounced the film, despite the fact that it did inordinately well at the box-office and earned him a tidy sum:

> *Because a lot of people expect to go see Casey Donovan in another* Boys in the Sand, *they want to see me in glossy sunshine and on the beach...and it's Casey Donovan in the johns, and it's very grubby. A lot of people are offended by it. They don't want to see that sort of aspect. Still, it's in its twelfth week....* [7]

Two days after shooting wrapped on *The Back Row*, *Captain Brasshound's Conversion* went on the road, with try-outs in Wilmington and Washington, and then a week in Toronto, Canada. Because of Ingrid Bergman's tight schedule, there were just sixteen performances in New York, but these were very well received—naturally, almost all of the plaudits going to the leading lady.

One of Casey's most esteemed clients at this time was the former actor-dancer-model William Como (1925-89), the editor of *After Dark*. Launched in May 1968, it had replaced *Ballroom Dance Magazine*, but covered all aspects of the performing arts with heavy emphasis on "eye candy"—hunky, frequently shirtless and near-nude men in homoerotic but inoffensive poses whose photographs graced the covers, interspersed with luminaries such as Maria Callas, Mae West, Robert Redford, Joan Crawford, and Paul Newman. In 1997, fourteen years after the magazine ceased publication, Daniel Harris observed:

It was one of the strangest reincarnations in journalistic history. Catering to musically-inclined blue-haired old ladies and golfers in Hush-Puppies, *Ballroom Dance Magazine* was a recreational journal for the geriatric set. It was out of the ashes of a periodical devoted to such topics as waltzes, rumbas and Turkey-Trots that *After Dark*, an audacious mass-market experiment in gay eroticism, arose like a phoenix in all of its subversive splendour. [8]

Como's targeted audience was singleton gays in the upper earnings bracket. His speciality was covering New York-based productions often shunned by his contemporaries: controversial musicals such as *Hair*, and obscure gay-themed plays and films. Though never classed as a gay magazine, there was also substantial coverage of gay guest-houses and hotels, restaurants, nightclubs, bars and bathhouses, but most especially gay movies, books, magazines, underwear and swimwear, and other products. The magazine famously promoted *The David Kopay Story*, within which the footballer came out as gay, the first American athlete to do so. Also promoted was an organization identified as "GSF", with the caption, "No Man Should Be Without A Man!" the editorial of which added, "If you would like to meet warm, sincere gay men (and women) who are interested in forming relationships, then it's about time you found out about GSF."

Wakefield Poole had little difficulty promoting Casey's work in *After Dark*—even *The Back Room* was advertised, sparing few details on the storyline.

Casey appeared in the February 1972 issue—a head shot which attracted the attention of Roy Blakely, the Oklahoma-born photographer who learned his craft while serving with the US Army during the 1950s, but on his discharge opted to pursue his other interest—ice-skating, touring with *Holiday on Ice* until 1967 when he began snapping the male physique and settled in New York. Blakely took several shots of Casey, naked from the pubes up, and one of these appeared in *After Dark*'s March issue, along with a brief editorial which erroneously stated that he had appeared in the stage play of *Dragula* at the Garrick Theater, and not the film.

Soon after this session, and finding a gap in his busy schedule, Casey arranged for him and his lover Donald to take a vacation to Fire Island, where they were to part-share a house with friends near where *Boys in the Sand* had been filmed. They had packed their suitcases when Casey received a call from the avant-garde director **Radley Metzger**. In 1961, Metzger (1929-2017) had founded Audubon Films with the distributor Ava Leighton, and among their acclaimed films as the decade closed were *Therese & Isabelle* (1968) and *Camille 2000* (1969). Acting on Jerry Douglas' recommendation Metzger offered Casey the male lead in the screen version of his off-Broadway play, *Score*, which had been staged at New York's Martinique Theatre between 28 October and 15 November 1971.

Of the original cast—Michael Beirne (Jack), Ben Wilson (Eddie), Lynn Swan (Betsy), Clair Wilbur (Elvira)—only the latter would appear in the film. It is believed that future superstar Sylvester Stallone, who played Mike, the telephone repairman, *wanted* to be in it, but Metzer considered him too "Queens New York raw" for the screen. *Score* was an example of the so-called "porn chic" phase of the early 1970s which included *The Devil In Miss Jones* and *Deep Throat*, but while this and Metzger's other films had explored heterosexuality, with the odd excursion into lesbianism, this would become the first non-X-rated film to have homosexual scenes. In January 2014, the director explained:

> *When I was coming of age, eroticism was always in films, but eroticism was punished. The promiscuous girl never got the leading man. The woman who sold her charms always had a bad fate. The good girl always achieves ends the bad girl never did. As a reaction to that, I tried to do the opposite. You could have a free attitude and behave in a free way, and not be punished....It didn't have to be tragedy. You could look at sex in a fun way. That was a personal thing, to work against the clichés in cinema when I was growing up.* [9]

No sooner had Casey signed the contract for the film—to be billed as Calvin Culver—than he was contacted by the Wilhelmina Agency, who had signed him up to model for **Valentino, in Italy,** with a series of engagements that would take immediate effect. The timing could not have been more perfect: he would fly to Rome, complete the assignment, then meet up with the cast and crew of *Score*—Radley Metzger was yet to decide where it would be filmed, other than it would be somewhere in Europe. Before he set off, Casey headed to Fire Island to take part along with four others in a fashion shoot for *After Dark*. Accompanying him were William Como, photographer Kenn Duncan, and fashion editor Roberta Burrows.

Duncan (1928-86) was one of the most celebrated artists of his day, working primarily for *After Dark* and *Vogue*, though his portraits also appeared regularly in *Time* and *Newsweek*. He photographed many Broadway plays such *Hair, Applause*, and *The Elephant Man*. His closest friends included Angela Lansbury, and Carol Channing. He is known to have had a fling with Casey at around the time of the photo-shoot. His pictures here are with actors Gene Vladimar and Bryce Holman, actress Laine Carlos, and ballerina Alexis Hoff. Casey was snapped at the Monster Restaurant wearing a Lew Magram butterfly-patterned kaftan, at the Beach Hotel wearing a Boutique St Tropez white safari-suit, and on the beach in Speedos and a P J Boutique "bathing-suit with braces"—which today would be called a mankini. When the others were not around, Duncan also photographed him hanging from a trapeze and wearing Speedos—and on a swing, naked and photographed from below.

Little is known of Casey's trip to Italy. In Rome he rented a room near the Spanish Steps, and when not working spent his leisure time catching up with friends and clients acquired during his last visit to the Eternal City. It is known that he spent a week at the villa of an Italian count, and several days with the dashing Prince Egon von Furstenberg, more of whom later—an idyll shattered by a call from Radley Metzger. *Score* was about to start shooting.

George Payne, Casey's love
interest in *The Back Row*.

The Back Row: having found the love
of his life, Casey is still cruising…

With Ingrid Bergman.

That *After Dark* cover…

With Laine Carlos.

The fashion shoot for *After* Dark: Casey, Laine
Carlos, Gene Vladimar and Alexis Hoff.

The fashion shoot for *After Dark...*
minus the clothes!

5: *Score*

Casey was the image of straight masculinity. He did not look like someone who would suck cock or throw his legs in the air. When he did, the gay audiences were surprised and gratified. Our fantasies were fulfilled. (Robert Richards)

Jerry Douglas' setting of the stage version of *Score* had been a tawdry New York tenement apartment. Radley Metzger, however, wanted a lavish location for the glamorous cast he had assembled. Initially, he plumped for the French Riviera, but as the cost of filming here for the nine weeks schedule would prove exorbitant, he settled for renting a house—the home of an absent high-ranking military official—in Bakar, near Ljubljana on the former Yugoslavia's beautiful Dalmatian Coast. Metzger had filmed his *Little Mother* here the previous year with Mark Damon, and now employed the same Yugoslav production team, headed by Branko Lustig, who later worked on *Gladiator* and *Schindler's List*. No one extant of the set knew *what* was being filmed, and everyone was paid well enough not to let on: Marshall Tito was still in power, and homosexuality very much frowned upon in this part of the world.

Gerald Grant (1940-93) was also recommended by Jerry Douglas, and Metzer had been impressed with Lynn Lowry's performance in the rushes he had seen for the yet to be released soft-porn romp, *Sugar Cookies*. For the part of Mike, the telephone repairman, he hired Carl Parker, a good-looking but hard-bitten thirty-something actor who had recently appeared in a series of "male chauvinist pig" cigarette commercials.

As the bigger names in the production, Casey and Lowry were paid the highest salaries, but *how* much they received was not made public. Though Gerald Grant was happy with this, Clair Wilbur (1933-2004) was not, and caused considerable tension on the set. According to Lowry, Carl Parker was also problematic, believing that if they were going to have sex in the film, they should prepare themselves for this by having sex away from the set! Casey, on the other hand, she adored and they remained good friends for the rest of his life, and unlike Parker she *had* wanted to get physical with him:

> *I really enjoyed getting to know him. We would go out to dinner together. We would hang out together because Gerry Grant and Claire would be doing scenes and we would have all this time...He was just a very gentle, sweet person. There were a couple of times when we were like, "What are we going to do today? We don't have anything to do? Shall we have sex, or something?" Cal would say, "You know, I'm gay!" He was gorgeous!* [1]

Casey later spoke of a "sexual experience" that had taken place, in Bakar at the Uvala Scott Hotel, with a female co-star—which could only have been Lowry or Claire Wilbur. This is not as improbable as it sounds: his first porn loops had seen him having penetrative sex with women—as opposed to the simulated sex of *Eleanor*—and in the not too distant future he would do so again. He recalled, of Yugoslavia, "There is great poverty in that country, but also great happiness."

There were two versions of the film: the "regular" one which had full-frontal nudity but no erections, and the seven minutes longer hard-core version where there is penetration and fellatio involving *only* the male characters, *and* with money-shots which did not make it to the finished print. As the Yugoslav cameraman refused to shoot these, Metzger personally took over the camera work. The scene with the women was filmed first, that with the men after Claire Wilbur left the country and returned to New York.

The action takes place in the mythical European city of Leisure (annoying pronounced *Leesure*), and there are shades of *Who's Afraid of Virginia Woolf?* (1966) with Wilbur and Grant replicating the older Elizabeth Taylor and Richard Burton, and Casey and Lowry resembling the mixed up George Segal and Sandy Denny characters—with the addition, of course, of a great deal of sex. Like the Taylor-Burton film, the action takes place over a twenty-four hour period.

Glamour photographer Jack (Grant) and his wife Elvira (Wilbur) have a strong and happy union, but like to "swing" and are unconventional—they have phallus-shaped candles and keep their marijuana inside a pepper-mill. Last night's adventure was something of a let-down, so today she has planned "Operation Music-Box". Cut to relative newlyweds 22-year-old [sic] Eddie (Casey) and Betsy (Lowry), just waking up. Betsy reaches under the covers, and

74

fondles Eddie. She gets him hard, but he does not wish to have sex with her—instead, he heads to the bathroom to masturbate. This was the very last sequence that Metzer filmed, he claimed because Casey had "saved himself" for a week "to shoot a big load", but the actual ejaculation shot, into the sink, was cut from the finished print.

Cut back to Elvira, awaiting a visit from her friend Betsy to make the final arrangements for their dinner-party tonight—and sabotaging the telephone in the hope of getting a randy repairman to come around and fix it, and maybe have a little fun. Betsy arrives, and they talk about sex. Elvira says that it took her a while to get used to Jack's swinging ways, of how he told her when they were first wed, "I'd climb upon a porcupine if it struck my fancy!" Mike the repairman turns up. He is a ruggedly handsome hunk and when Elvira scalds him with coffee he whips off his T-shirt to reveal a pleasantly hairy chest, but an unattractive hirsute back. He and Elvira have sex on the rug while Betsy, a naïve Catholic girl who might not even have done this with Eddie unless under the covers, moves around studying them intently each time they change position—finally grabbing a camera and clicking the shutter as they climax.

Cut to the party. Now aware of what might happen, Betsy feigns a headache but is persuaded to turn up. Eddie tells Jack that he only drinks milk because since the age of fifteen he has had an ulcer—adding that alcohol makes him carefree, though he does not refuse the glass of Scotch offered him. Jack admires the ring on his little finger. Casey wears this in some of his films, but his character here thinks that it is "queer faggoty". He and Betsy bicker a lot, but settle down when joints are passed around. When Eddie sees what the hunk is wearing on the cover of one of Jack's gay magazines, he announces that he always wanted to be a cowboy, while Jack says he always wanted to be a sailor. Betsy adds how she once had hopes of becoming a model. This leads to everyone playing dress-up. Jack strips naked and puts on a sailor suit—effecting the film's first full-frontal nude shot—and Eddie draws a tattoo on his arm to complete the look. Betsy puts on a skimpy lace ensemble which makes her look like a hooker. Mocking Betsy's religion, Elvira dresses as a nun. Eddie is reluctant to undress because he is shy of doing so in front of another man, but does so and reveals all in a stunning full-frontal close up. Few screen cowboys have looked quite so amazing. After dinner, Jack and Elvira discuss tactics. All summer they have been in competition with each other to see who can have the most same-sex conquests, and the wager they made six months ago ends in two hours' time, at midnight. They agree that if Elvira can seduce Betsy into having sex with her by then, *he* will promise *not* to seduce Eddie so that she can also have sex with him. Then Eddie and Betsy start arguing again when, under the influence, he says that he looks like a real cowboy, and Betsy snipes that he is a native New Yorker pretending to be something he is not—obviously hinting that he may be gay. She further ridicules him for having no chest hair while Jack is superbly hirsute—as a result of this scene being a pivotal part of the plot and the fact that Eddie is *so* youthful looking that he is still asked to show his identity when going into bars, Radley Metzger had instructed Casey to shave his entire torso, something he was unhappy about and which his fans considered sacrilege.

Leaving Elvira to get on with seducing Betsy, Jack takes Eddie to a bar to get him in the mood, while Betsy explains to Elvira what happened this morning—how she walked into the bathroom and caught Eddie taking himself in hand. She adds how everyone told her they should never have married, even her brother who was Eddie's best friend—another gay hint.

The wives and husbands pair off—Betsy and Elvira to the bedroom, Jack and a slightly inebriated Eddie to the downstairs den—where they express dissatisfaction with their spouses. Eddie reveals that he was Betsy's brother's closest friend, suggesting they may have been lovers. Betsy thinks that something "may happen" between her and Elvira, and says "fuck" for the first time—Jerry Douglas making a point that even good Catholic girls curse. Jack tells Eddie of Elvira's nymphomania, that before they married she told him, a near-repetition of the earlier line and a faux-pas on the part of the scriptwriter, "Jack, I'd hop in the sack with a porcupine if it struck my fancy." All four sniff poppers, Eddie agrees to sleep over, and sex takes place with the camera zipping back and forth between the couples as they get increasingly more intimate. Eddie confesses that he is unhappy with his lot, telling Jack, "When you hate to go to work on a morning and you hate to come home at night, there's not a lot left." Betsy tells Elvira of how she found Eddie's stash of gay porn magazines, and that

77

she is sure that he *wants* to go to bed with a man, though he may not yet have done so. Eddie confesses to Jack that he and a male friend "messed around" when he was fifteen—at around the time he got his ulcer. The couples undress, but while the sex between the women is simulated, in the hard-core version that between the men is real. In extreme close-up they masturbate each other, perform fellatio and sixty-nine, and Jack penetrates Eddie who, high on marijuana, fantasises that it is Betsy, wearing a collar and leash, who is penetrating him with a strap-on.

Morning comes and Elvira and Jack declare themselves even where their wager was concerned. Eddie cannot remember what has transpired, and flinches when Jack tries to kiss him. He and Betsy bicker again, then realise that they have found themselves sexually. Mike arrives, meets Jack and confesses that has never had sex with a man, but will try anything once. He, Jack, Betsy and Elvira get naked on the rug, but Mike shrugs off Jack's advances. Then Eddie comes downstairs. He wants to go bowling with Eddie and Betsy—nothing to do with the sport, as he and Mike have clicked already. "How do you think we'll do in the Olympics?" he asks, as the three of them grab the pepper-mill and rush off, while the voice-over announces that Big Bad Wolf (Mike) has made friends with Prince Charming (Eddie). The film ends with Elvira and Jack heading for the local bistro and plotting their next adventure—with the hunky young waiter.

Score had a staggered release, Metzger claimed because *Deep Throat*, released the previous year, was still monopolising the market, and cinemagoers

78

were not yet ready for bisexual adult entertainment. It opened in Quebec in February 1974, and in Los Angeles two months later—when special guests were presented with popper-holders embossed with the film's title. New York audiences saw it for the first time in the August, and though it was not a tremendous box-office hit at the time, it became so when restored and is now regarded as a classic. *In Touch*'s film critic enthused:

> Straight audiences are being treated to a special joyous delight. Considering that until now homosexuals only took prat falls and did Step-'n-Fetch-it routines, the film is easily classified as *revolutionary*....With fiendish humour Metzger has not only presented straight porn showing two men engaged in sexual play, but his leading hetero is none other than Casey Donovan, aka Cal Culver....It is entertaining and enjoyable, filled with sophisticated humour dependent upon an abundance of subtle innuendo and side glance. It is well written, well balanced and witty, a play with some exceptionally fine performances. It is a fine, successful achievement on all counts. See it. [2]

Casey returned to New York. Donald, his lover, had taken umbrage with him for foregoing their holiday on Fire Island to go jetting off to Yugoslavia, and had moved on. On the positive side, the photo-shoot for *After Dark* had been published in the magazine's July issue with Kenn Duncan's shot of Laine Carlos on the beach with a serious-looking, smooth-chested

Casey—looking stunning in his mankini—on the cover. The piece by Roberta Burrows was headed, "And They All Went to the Beach", and observed:

> Young stars and promising starlets, disciplined ballerinas, the future faces of stage and screen. Young disciplined performers taking their winter bodies out of hibernation....Healthy. Fit. Real people in motion. Such are the bathing beauties this summer of '72. [3]

The feature applauded the achievements of the five young people featured in Kenn Duncan's picture-spread. Russian-born model Gene Vladimir had the title-role in a major film, *Bonner* (which was never made), and was considering roles in four more big-budget productions which also never saw the light of day. Bryce Holman and Laine Carlos had also been pencilled in to make major films, which never happened. Alexis Hoff was a ballerina with Dallas Civic Opera. Of the quintet, only Hoff and Casey would leave their mark on the entertainment world. Of Casey, fashion editor Roberta Burrows enthused:

> Cal Culver has appeared with Ingrid Bergman in the touring and Broadway production of *Captain Brasshound's Conversion*. Though *It Ain't Easy* is the title of his next movie, it hardly describes his active acting and modelling careers, both of which come quite easily. He is presently in Yugoslavia playing one of the leads in Radley Metzger's film, *Score*. [4]

William Como had called Casey in Rome. Under the heading, "Yeah, But Can He Do Dialogue?" he wrote in a last minute addition to Burrow's feature:

> "I don't have any hang-ups about who and what I am," says super-handsome Cal Culver. And apparently Mother Nature approves. A handful of important modelling assignments, a variety of short theatre stints, and a skinflick or two are propelling Monday's child along a storybook path towards the land of Oz. He gathers admirers easily along the way...."Yeah, but can he do dialogue?" one lady said to another, after seeing *Boys*. Mother Nature and I are betting that he can. **[5]**

Asked the secret of his success, Casey explained:

> *I think you've got to like yourself to become a success, and I'm very confident and honest about me. I can never put down having done those three films* [Boys in the Sand, Casey, The Back Row] *because they were a fantastic chance for me to play in front of a camera. I've learned so much about myself from those films—the little subtleties of expression with my face and body. It's difficult to let yourself go—to be relaxed and natural. I try to concentrate on the action first, the camera second. I'm very proud of* Boys, *because I think it's a very beautiful film and one of the best of its kind that's ever been made. It's kind of a classic.* **[6]**

And, Como wanted to know, what did the future hold for Casey Donovan, or Cal Culver, whichever name he opted to use for his next project? Casey told him:

> *Raymond St Jacques wants me to play a role in his new film,* Book of Numbers. *He told me, "You have a charisma that Robert Redford had when he first started. You've really got to get it together and get into films. It's where you belong."* [7]

In fact, it was Ingrid Bergman who first made the comparison between Casey and Robert Redford, to a Wilmington journalist during the tour of *Captain Brasshound's Conversion*. Raymond St Jacques (1930-90) was the first African-American to play a regular major role in a television western series when cast as Simon Blake in *Rawhide*. *Book of Numbers* was scheduled to start shooting as soon as Casey had finished his next film, now retitled *Fun and Games*, though it would still be released in Europe as *It Ain't Easy*. His comment to Casey about "getting it together" came with an ultimatum: that he should give up porn if he wanted the part in the film, set in Arkansas during the Depression. St Jacques was being hypocritical, for he had gushed over *Boys in the Sand*. Casey saw no reason why he should not do porn *and* legitimate films. So far he had fared well in both, and he turned St Jacques down. He was next approached by Robert Fryer, and offered a part in *The King Must Die*, based on Mary Renault's novel, and which told the story of Theseus. Fryer was hoping to cast Maggie Smith as one of the leads—he had co-produced her recent *The Prime of Miss Jean Brodie*. The production fell through. Ten years later, Casey would remember this and tell film historian Vito Russo:

> *Perhaps I was naïve, but it was a rude awakening for me to find out that Hollywood is one of the most closeted and hypocritical cultural centres in the world. I learned that an openly gay actor like myself was not welcome to gay directors and producers who believe it is essential to keep their sexuality a secret. Once an actor has made a porn movie, it's very difficult to cross over. And it has nothing to do with how much talent one has. It's all about how an actor is perceived and prejudged. In a limited sphere, my films made me famous, but in another sense they were a handicap.* **[8]**

Meanwhile, Casey made *It Ain't Easy/Fun and Games*, a sexploitation spoof directed by Mervyn Nelson. His co-star was Alice Spivak, but it was he, as serial philanderer Bob Cartwright, whose picture appeared on the playbills—leering lasciviously at a pretty blonde. The storyline centered around a swinging couple—pretty much how Eddie and Betsy had become by the end of *Score*—who respond to an ad in *Screw* magazine in the hope of having, well, fun and games. The tagline said it all:

> Interested? Swinging couple seeking broadminded men, women and couples for 'Fun and Games'.

Casey was however beginning to regret that fame had to a certain extent restricted his freedom of movement—that he could no longer socialise the way he had in the past, or even sometimes go for a stroll without someone walking up to him. While confessing that recognition had been incredible the first weekend after his return from Yugoslavia, he now admitted that the novelty had worn off:

> *It was like being a new face but not exactly a new face....It was really frightening. I went through the whole recognition trip, people doing numbers and people sort of stopping and doing double takes. And I thought, "Wow, now I really realise why people in Hollywood want their privacy, why they don't go out in public, why they don't want to sign autographs, why they want to be left alone"....Sometimes it's a great deal of fun, and sometimes it can be a bummer. Sometimes it's annoying, you don't want to be bothered. And I really realised what a price you have to pay to your public. And I thought. "Jesus, if this is happening to me, think what Bette Davis has gone through all these years....the letters and the phone calls and the kooks that come by!"* **[9]**

It amused him when people meeting him for the first time always remarked how pleasant he was:

> *I met a lot of people in films who were curious to meet me...and find out what I was*

84

like. We'd talk for a while and they'd say, "You know, you're very nice. I didn't think you'd be this nice. I thought you'd be, I don't know, a creep or whatever." People had some conception that I would be sort of a cunt or something, that I would be very offensive, a hustler type. And I thought, "Well, why shouldn't I be nice? I'm a nice guy. **[10]**

Casey was depicted cosying up to another pretty blonde on the cover of the 27 November 1972 issue of *Newsweek*, under the heading, "The New Sex Therapy". It was the magazine's second-best selling issue of the year. The photograph by J. Frederick Smith—of a gay man looking very content with his woman—did not bear testament to what the feature proclaimed, for if anyone did *not* have any problems with sex, it was Casey:

> At least half of the married couples in the United States have problems with sex. Now, as a result of the pioneering work of Masters and Johnson, sexual therapy clinics offering simple, fast cures are rapidly spreading across the country. But some critics raise moral questions about the clinics' workshop techniques, and many psychiatrists believe that simple sex therapy leaves deeper problems untouched... **[11]**

In December 1972, Casey appeared on the cover of *After Dark* for the third time that year—a head-and-shoulders shot by Jack Mitchell. The feature within announced that he had been signed to play opposite

Maggie Smith in *The King Must Die*, albeit that the deal had fallen through.

In January 1973, Wakefield Poole relocated to Los Angeles, and Casey moved into the West Side duplex apartment he vacated, a vast place with 24-foot high rooms which he filled with tropical plants, and which set him back a cool $450 a month. An early visitor was Stephen F. Zito, who observed:

> Welcome to Cal's world, and to its main attraction, Cal Culver, aka Casey Donovan. It's a world where the good things are a hoot, the bad ones tacky. It is a world of flash and filigree, a world of seeing and, more important, being seen, a world that is filled to the top with people who are inordinately pleased to have the pleasure of Cal Culver's company. [12]

Alice Spivak (right) and two lovelies vie for
Casey's sexual favours in *Fun & Games* (1973).

CAL CULVER
IS COMING!...

this fall in
"SCORE"

a new
motion picture
directed by
Radley Metzger.

with Claire Wilbur / Lynn Lowry / Gerald Grant
Carl Parker / screenplay by Jerry Douglas
Eastmancolor / an [ ] Audubon Films Release

The pre-publicity poster for *Score* (released 1974)

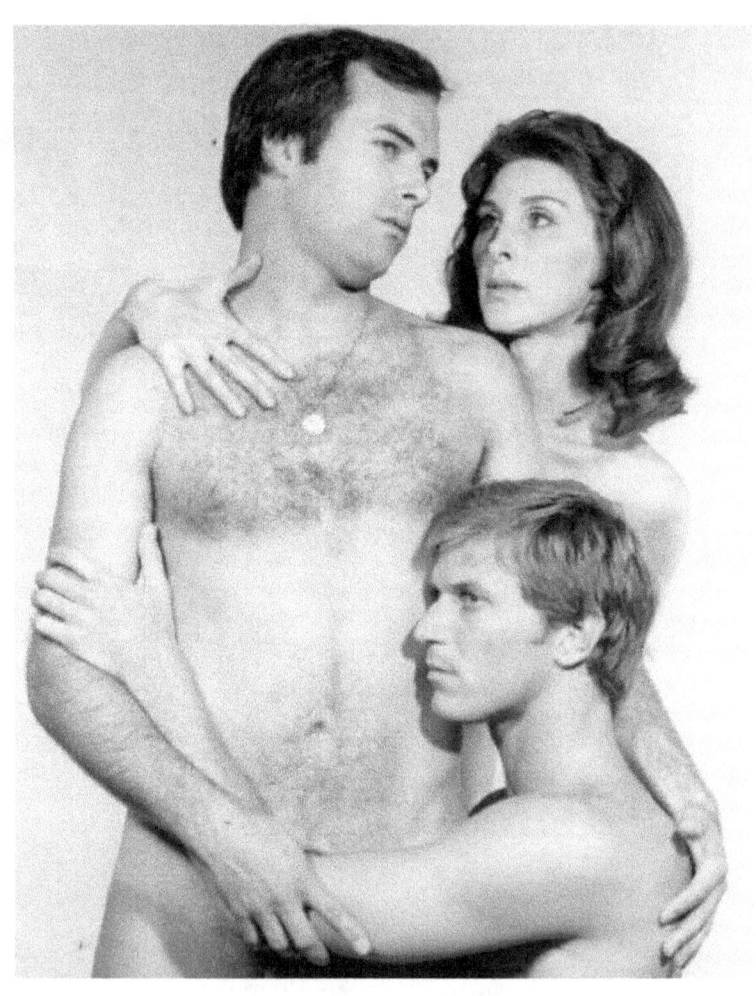

Casey, Gerald Grant and Claire Wilbur.

Claire Wilbur, Carl Parker, Lynne Lowry and
Casey on the set of *Score*.

Eddie/Casey, looking a little naïve…

...though not quite so naïve once he gets into his
cowboy gear!

Will *it* happen with Jack?

You bet! With Gerald Grant.

The Los Angeles premiere of *Score*: Gerry Grant,
Claire Wilbur, Casey and Radley Metzger.

Playing it straight with an unidentified
blonde on the cover of *Newsweek*.

6: Tom Tryon & *Tubstrip*

I tried to maintain separate names and identities at first: "Casey Donovan" did the gay stuff, "Cal Culver" did the other stuff, the legitimate plays and the modeling. It got increasingly confusing if not schizophrenic. Besides, the secret could not be perpetuated endlessly. Now it doesn't matter who knows who I am or what name they call me as long as they call me. (Casey)

Casey's roommate in his new home was Jake Getty, a close friend of whom little is known. At the end of the month the pair threw a "rent" house-warming party, where each guest had to pay at the door—a nominal fee of one dollar. Almost 500 people turned up, and celebrity guests included Sylvia Miles, Uva Harden, Rex Reed—and Richard Deacon, the prissy actor from *The Dick Van Dyke Show* and numerous television sitcoms who brought along the former actor Tom Tryon. Casey had met him three years earlier, during a theatrical jaunt with Donald, when neither had taken much notice of the other. Now, it was love at first sight. Tryon stayed over after the party, setting in motion an incredibly stormy, and on Tryon's part violent relationship.

Tom Tryon (1926-91) was a strapping, 6 foot 3 inch brute of a man. Born in Hartford, Connecticut, he served with the US Navy in the Pacific from 1943-6, and later attended and graduated from Yale University. He studied acting at New York's Neighbourhood Playhouse, and in 1952 appeared on

93

Broadway in *Wish You Were Here,* with Jack Cassidy. Television roles followed, mostly in westerns including bit-parts in *Wagon Train* and *Frontier*, before he was signed up to play the lead in Disney's *Texas John Slaughter*. His film career kicked off in 1956 with a starring role in Michael Curtiz' crime drama, *The Scarlet Hour*, but his most famous role was in *The Cardinal* (1963)—a hugely successful film which earned him a Golden Globe nomination, but a harrowing experience from which he never recovered. It was directed by Otto Preminger, known for frequently giving his actors a hard time on the set. Halfway through shooting, he lost his temper with Tryon and fired him, only to reinstate him one hour later when convinced that he had been sufficiently humiliated. Then on he became increasing disillusioned with Hollywood, and retired in 1969 to begin a new career as a best-selling novelist, specialising in horror and insisting that henceforth he should only be addressed as Thomas. When he became involved with Casey he was working on *Harvest Home*, which told of pagan rituals in New England—five years later this would be adapted into a television mini-series, *The Dark Secret of Harvest Home*, starring Bette Davis.

Psychologically, Casey and Tom Tryon could not have been more ill-matched. The 17-year age-gap aside, whereas Casey had never been in the closet, Tryon was paranoid about his sexuality becoming public knowledge, which begs the question why he became involved with one of the world's most renowned porn stars in the first place. Though billed as Calvin Culver in stage and soft-core productions, in magazine interviews and features, both aspects of his career were openly and honestly discussed. Whereas Casey was known for his fun-loving, sunny disposition—there is no record of his ever arguing or fighting with *anyone*, even when his patience had been tested to the limit—Tryon was surly and bad-tempered, especially when he had been drinking, or when suffering from writers' block. In 1955, he had entered into a "lavender" marriage with stockbroker's daughter Ann Noyes, the former wife actor-producer Thomas Ewing Noyes. They had divorced three years later, whence she had reverted to her former married name. There had been several male partners since this time, all of them treated badly, but Casey is believed to have been the one he loved the most, even though his behaviour towards him was reprehensible much of the time. The blogger "Mr. Breckenridge" aptly observed, sixteen years after Tryon's death from cancer of the stomach and spine:

> Whether Tryon kept a journal or wrote of his own issues with his sexuality is unknown. Was he happy and satisfied with the way he lived? Did he ever let his parents know, or did they even have the kind of relationship that allowed such intimate topics?...His sexual orientation must have been well-known, probably one of the reasons he was harassed by dictators like Preminger. He was well-spoken and extremely handsome, with a deep voice and strong features. But just how "masculine" he was in person is a matter of opinion and probably lost in the murky annals of the celluloid closet. [1]

Neither were the pair faithful to one another. It had never been in Casey's nature to be monogamous, and nothing would change on this score. Tryon had a lover "on the sideline"—Trinidad-born actor and dancer Clive Clerk (1945-2000), who in 1964 had also appeared with Rock Hudson and Doris Day in *Send Me No Flowers*. In a very small world, Clerk shared Tryon with the dancer and choreographer Michael Bennett (1943-87), best remembered for *A Chorus Line*, in which Clerk was an original cast member. And though Tryon may not have known, Clerk and Bennett were also sleeping with Casey!

Both Clerk and Casey held on to Tryon and put up with his tantrums not just because of his alleged voracious sexual appetite but because if his valuable show business connections. After dancing in innumerable revues and in NBC's *Hullabaloo*, Bennet had enjoyed his first major success as a choreographer on Broadway with *Promises, Promises* (1968) which had a pop score by Burt Bacharach and Hal David. This had run for over 1,200 performances. Since then he had worked with Katherine Hepburn and Stephen Sondheim, and was currently involved with the Dorothy Fields-Cy Coleman musical, *Seesaw*, scheduled to open at New York's Mark Hellinger Theatre in March. For now, Bennett came up with an idea for a musical to be written especially for Casey, who recalled:

> *It's incredible, just brilliant, completely original. He has become very kind of infatuated with me. He just felt that something was going to happen to me, and wanted to help me make it work....So I have*

been sort of collaborating with him, giving him a lot of ideas for it, but my job is to really get my voice together and learn to tap dance. [2]

There was of course nothing wrong with Casey's singing voice. The project never materialised, though he did not remain idle for very long. Ellis Rabb (1930-98) was an actor-producer-playwright and artistic director of the Phoenix Repertory Company, and was casting for the smaller parts in an avant-garde production of Shakespeare's *The Merchant of Venice*, to be staged at the Lincoln Center's Vivian Beaumont Theatre. The principal players were his ex-wife Rosemary Harris, Philip Bosco and Christopher Walken. There would be forty-four performances. The first preview took place on 18 February 1973, and the play closed on 7 April—though it played to a packed house every performance, Rabb and Harris's next venture, *A Streetcar Named Desire*, was scheduled to open two weeks later.

To say that this production was different may be an understatement. This particular Venice contained decadent beaches and bars, and Belmont was a millionaire's yacht moored in a lagoon populated with all manner of rich folk. Bastiano and Antonio (Walken, Joseph Sommer) were over-the-top-camp homosexuals, Portia (Harris) was a middle-aged lush, and Shylock spoke incomprehensible Yiddish. Casey, billed as Calvin Culver, understudied the part of Leonardo, Bassanio's manservant who was played by Robert Phalen. Additionally, he had four "ensemble" parts. At one stage of the production he appeared as a youth, wearing drag and on stilts. More controversially he played Jesus Christ—wearing a crown of thorns, and a chain-mail posing-pouch which barely contained his assets. Even so, it was all in good taste and never irreverent, so much so that Casey's mother, his brother Duane and his former teacher Helen Van Fleet were special guests at the opening night. Fortunately for them, they were not present when Casey invited the entire cast back to his apartment, where the entertainment included a special screening of *Boys in the Sand*.

But if audiences loved the play, the critics did not. Clive Barnes wrote in *The New York Times*:

> An opening fanfare of jazz, a Pucci and Gucci glint, and a Venice observed by Fellini and Visconti—these are the attitudes indicated by Ellis Rabb, the producer of *The Merchant of Venice*...Here, to pace Shakespeare's tale of love, destiny and usury in contemporary Cinzano-sipping Venice is to push credulity to the limit. Mr. Rabb has gone to Shakespeare with a knife so sharp that Shylock himself might have envied it. [3]

John Symon observed in *New York Magazine*:

> Ellis Rabb's production of *The Merchant of Venice* might be described as rock bottom for the doomed Repertory Theatre of the Lincoln Centre if anything as viscous, pulpy and nerveless deserved the epithet "rock"...Venetian society now consists of campy homosexuals and idle tourists, and an

honest, noble Jew, Shylock…It would be unfair to many other directors to call Ellis Rabb the worst in America, but he is certainly the most perverse. [4]

The success of *Boys in the Band* and *Score*—and the notoriety of *The Back Row*, cost Casey dearly. Thus far, he had managed to be in control of two careers: the handsome model and legitimate stage actor that women wanted and men envied, most of them unaware of his sexuality—and the object of desire which had started out almost with an air of innocence in *Casey*, and progressed into the "sex-pig" applauded by Jerry Douglas.

The theatre community had never been less than gay-friendly, or at least certainly more gay-tolerant than the film world, and all of those that Casey had worked with in both genres had known that Calvin Culver and Casey Donovan were one and the same, and accepted this because, professionally, the one had never interfered with the other. The modelling world was another matter. The first to submit a complaint to Wilhelmina was the director of Arrow Shirts, causing the company to dispense with his services. *The New York Times Sunday Supplement* were next, followed by Valentino, who had planned including Casey in their next major American and European advertising campaigns.

Casey was understandably offended. He was unique—and remains so today—in that he was the only A-lister porn star to successfully transfer to mainstream films and back again, *and* to keep working on the stage. Therefore, he saw no reason why he should not continue doing both. And now he was once again thinking of giving up porn:

If someone comes along and legitimises my career, there's no use going backward. And I feel that doing porno's going backwards. It's not going to advance me. My agent just came back from California, and people do talk about me. I'm sort of an interesting commodity, but a lot of people are afraid to take a chance with me because I've done the porno films. That's why I don't want to do any more because I'm really afraid of jeopardising, now that I do have a legitimate film career going, and I don't want to jeopardise any good modelling job. **[5]**

He reiterated this point, telling Allan Leopold:

I had planned on doing a book called Letters to Casey, *with half text and half pictures because I was flooded with fan letters after* Boys in the Sand, *but I'm trying to tone down the whole image right now rather than adding fuel to the fire. At one time I was literally going to kill off Casey Donovan. The week* The Back Row *opened in New York, I wanted to take out an obit in Variety to put "In Memoriam Casey Donovan", and the date. But I decided better not kill off the goose that laid the golden egg. I might need Casey again! I don't know how much there is left of him in my future but on still moonlit nights when the wolf howls plaintively, a distinct possibility persists...that I might just descend my cellar stairs and start those test-tubes bubbling again!* [6]

To this end, when *The Merchant of Venice* closed, Casey responded to a call from Sal Mineo, who in the wake of a career hiatus had taken to producing and directing stage plays. In 1969, he had directed a Los Angeles production of the gay-themed *Fortune and Men's Eyes* featuring himself and Don Johnson, unknown at the time. This had included a graphic, extended prison rape scenario which had not gone down too well with the critics. Casey, in his Calvin Culver guise, was invited to audition for a part in Mineo's forthcoming off-Broadway production of *The Children's Mass,* by Frederick Combs, who had appeared in the stage and film versions of *Boys in the Band*, and was now trying his hand at play writing. This was scheduled to open at the Theatre de Lys on 5 May. Casey was successful in acquiring the part of Dutchie, and flung himself into learning his lines at home, with Mineo and Tom Tryon putting him through his paces. Much was made of the casting, which was announced in *After Dark* and several tabloid newspapers.

Casey and Mineo were among the guests invited to *After Dark*'s annual Ruby Awards ceremony, at New York's Delmonaco Hotel on 23 April, where Bette Midler was presented with the Entertainer of the Year Award. Here, he rubbed shoulders with Ethel Merman, Mick Jagger, Carrie Fisher, Ann Miller and dozens of other luminaries. Then, five days into rehearsals, Mineo fired him and replaced him with Gary Sandy, seemingly without giving him an explanation.

Casey had always been aware of his own value, and when the play bombed after just seven performances, he was not surprised:

A lot of people are going to be very disappointed, because of course I was in the big ad in After Dark. *They realised when they let me go that they were losing a great box-office potential—because you know my name has a certain draw and was going to sell tickets. Anyway, it's very chic this season to have your contract terminated. Everyone I talked to—agents and people who read the play and whatever—they all said they were glad I wasn't doing it after all. It's probably the best thing that happened to me, because evidently it's just not working. If it wasn't meant to be, it wasn't meant to be.* **[7]**

After Dark's Robb Baker, fervently denounced it:

The show pretty much falls apart, a sketchy plot bogged down with muddled religiosity, one-dimensional characterisations, and even two young children on the stage...I was also irritated by the ploy of having what was basically a gay theme filtered through the viewpoint of a playwright-character who happens to be "respectfully" straight. Didn't that kind of normality-by association liberalisation go out with 1950s attitudes towards Negroes and other nice quiet minority groups? **[8]**

Casey's feelings were hurt when, soon after the play closed, he learned that Mineo had told friends that he had dropped him from the play because, in his "professional" opinion, he could not act. According to one source, who asked not to be named:

> *Mineo broadcast to all and sundry that Cal was a useless actor, incapable of learning his lines. Nothing could have been further from the truth. Mineo wanted Cal to hop on to the casting couch, and also boasted about that. I'm sure that they would have ended up having sex at some stage, had they gone out on a date or something like that. But being expected to drop his pants to get a part was not Cal's style. He refused, and Mineo took offence and felt humiliated at being rejected. He fired him, then made up a story.* [9]

Salvation came with a phone call from Casey's friend Jerry Douglas, who without even requiring him to audition invited him to appear in the Los Angeles production of *Tubstrip*, a gay play he had written under the pseudonym A. J. Kronengold, and which would be directed by him as Doug Richards, the name he had adopted for *The Back Row*. The setting was a simple one: a group of gay men, in varying stages of nudity, gather in a bathhouse to discuss their lives and put the world to rights.

Tubstrip had opened in August 1973 at New York's Mercer Arts Theatre, with Gerald Grant— Casey's co-star in *Score*—heading the credits with Jamie Gillis, more of whom later. Days into the run, the production—along with the Mercer company's

One Flew Over the Cuckoo's Nest—had been forcibly closed when the adjacent Broadway Central Hotel had collapsed, rendering the area unsafe. Douglas had attempted to find another New York theatre to take his play, without success. Then at the end of September, by way of Douglas' tagline for the play, the *Los Angeles Times* announced:

> "The misadventures of eight boys and a dirty old man whose lives cross during one long evening at a Manhattan bath house" is coming to the Bitter End West on October 16. However, be informed that it is a show involving "extensive nudity" and "x-rated language"—their terms. **[10]**

The Bitter End West, on Santa Monica Blvd, was being refurbished for the occasion. Of the original cast, Gerald Grant was retained as sadistic leather man Tony, and Casey contracted to play Brian, the sympathetic bathhouse towel-boy. Jim Cassidy (1943-2013) a popular blond porn star and Colt model who as Rick Cassidy appeared mostly in heterosexual films, shared equal billing with Casey.

The play was an immediate hit with Los Angeles audiences. J. Moriarty enthused in *The Advocate*:

> It's erotic, bold, wild, and very often genuinely funny. Onstage, what the audience is seeing is what they're getting—plenty! The sexual energy that *Tubstrip* generates could knock out the energy crisis....It makes absolutely no concessions to the straight or uptight gay sensibility....The much-heralded

104

Calvin Culver (Casey Donovan) does okay for the pouting towel boy, but oddly enough he never once (at least at the preview) flashed a frontal view. [11]

Gerald Grant and the overtly-buffed Jim Cassidy may have received more critical accolades than the just "okay" Casey, but *he* was the one audiences were really interested in, and his presence brought revenue to the box-office. He alone was the reason for the play's run to be extended several times. A month into the run, Jim Cassidy left the production, resulting in Casey's name alone heading the credits.

Casey appeared to have broken his promise not to do any more porn, when an announcement appeared in *The Advocate*, on the eve of his thirtieth birthday:

Cal will be in Hollywood for the summer in the stage hit, *Tubstrip*, at the Hollywood Centre Theatre, so his days are free to do other work, if he desires. Cal acknowledged that he has been approached to do a film while he's here, but so far it's only in the talking stage. [12]

There were several legitimate film offers, but all of these fell through. Casey also appears to have revised his opinion of the casting-couch, as Jake Getty explained:

All it took was for someone to praise Cal, to tell him that he was going to be the next Tab Hunter or Robert Redford. He loved the praise. It was what he wanted to hear, and he believed it. It made Cal easy to manipulate.

A business lunch, a half hour of bullshit talk, and down went the pants. Once he'd been had, the film man's mission was accomplished, and Cal would have to wait until the next one came along. [13]

Finally, Wakefield Poole called Casey and asked him to appear in his next film, *Moving*, seeing as they were both in Hollywood. Since *Boys in the Sand*, Poole and his producer Marvin Shulman had made two films which, despite positive reviews, had not proved successful. *Bijou* starred Bill Harrison as a construction worker who, when he witnesses a car crash and finds the female victim's handbag, gets invited to her club—Bijou—and enters a weird world where fantasies become real. This had been followed with *The Bible*, a heterosexual exercise comprising a trio of Old Testament stories focusing on Adam and Eve, Bathsheba, and Delilah. The film was criticised for having a circumcised Adam (Bo White), and *The Devil in Miss Jones* star Georgina Spelvin (as Bathsheba) *not* engaged in pornography.

In many respects, though it has its moments of intense beauty, *Moving* is very unpleasant in parts. Gone is the romanticism and mystique of *Boys in the Sand*, the tongue-in-cheek humour of *Casey*, the loveable sex-pig of *The Back Room*. It was also the first film where Casey appears in just one segment, as opposed to having each one centered around him, with a continuing story.

Poole confirmed that with cash in short supply, the film was shot on a budget of just $4,800—though Casey's salary was never specified, unless he really did work for nothing, as he had been more than willing to do with *Boys in the Sand*. In the two loops where he does not appear, this lack of funds shows. Neither was the 8mm film made to be shown in the cinema, but to be sold by mail order. It was shot at a large house in the Hollywood Hills, owned by (unnamed) friends of Casey who, as with Poole's first film, stipulated that he could film anywhere in the grounds or around the pool, so long as he did not film the house itself.

Casey's 22-minutes segment, *House for Sale* opens with him arriving at the property in Beverly Hills that he is interested in buying. He looks dapper in his Arrow check shirt and tight-fitting denims, and as he strides through the greenery there are shades of *Boys in the Sand*. As with the earlier film, there is a classical music soundtrack, and no dialogue. In the hot-house he sees Brazilian bear Val Martin looking at him, and is sufficiently interested to fantasize about them getting intimate. To describe Martin as unattractive is an understatement. This really is a case of Beauty being rough-handled by The Beast. He has an unkempt beard and pock-marked face, and to confirm his own boast that he was a married heterosexual wears his wedding-ring. He is reputed to be thirty-three, but looks a good deal older. Not only does he fail to climax in the segment, despite Casey's sterling efforts to arouse him he does not even get an erection, whereas Casey remains hard throughout. As a preliminary to the sex we see them in the court playing tennis, Casey in a white Speedo and Martin wearing a jock-strap. Next we see them at the poolside where Martin is on a sun-lounger, and Casey facing him across the pool. Each time the camera cuts from one to the other they are wearing less, until both are naked, but with Martin keeping on his boots. Casey dives into the pool and swims across to his conquest where, brooking no delay, he fellates him. Next, Martin removes his boots, and uses their laces as makeshift cock-straps. What follows is acrobatic on Casey's part, lewd where Martin is concerned and was to have ended with Casey getting fisted—like the brief penetration scene, this is simulated. Even so, it does not make for comfortable viewing, which was why this and the third segment of the film was heavily cut before going on release. Wakefield Poole observed:

> Val was into fisting, which was becoming more and more popular, but Cal wasn't about to let that happen on film....There's an indication and an effort on their part to make that happen, which I put into the film, but it was never accomplished. Cal's struggle to let it happen or should I say, to not let it happen, is the main action of the segment. His desire and resistance to Val's urges gave me the tension I needed. It became a competition between Cal and Casey. [14]

A pleasing coda to this scene occurred the following year when, according to Poole, Chanel replicated a part of it for a television commercial:

> Cal at one point imagines Val at the opposite end of the pool. Cal dives into the pool, and swims under water to the edge of the pool to

where Val is in a deck chair. Then he rises
out of the water holding on to the edge of
the pool. It was a strong sexual image, and it
worked. [15]

There *was* a commercial for Chanel 5 made at the
time, directed by Ridley Scott, and the swimmer
does look like Casey. In the deckchair however is
not a gay porno star—this would not have got past
the censor have back then—but a beautiful woman.

In the second segment of the film, *Room for Rent,*
Burt Edouards and Curt Gerard rent a motel room
on Sunset Boulevard to have pedestrian sex. In the
third, *House for Rent*, a take on Bertolucci's recent
Last Tango in Paris, Peter Fisk plays out a fantasy
scenario with Tom Wright in Wakefield Poole's
apartment, of which the least said the better. It is
extreme, if not utterly repulsive to even the hardest
of hardcore enthusiasts and certainly not for those
with fickle stomachs.

Tom Tryon was displeased with Casey for making
Moving, but tolerated it because the film would not
be shown in cinemas. *Erotikus* was another matter.
This was a cobbled together documentary by Vydio
Phylms, made to be shown on cable television, prior
to which it premiered in *two* New York cinemas on
15 August 1973 in a blaze of publicity. Narrating
was Fred Halsted, who masturbates between the
various segments—though it is not his penis which
provides the money-shot at the end, to the closing
bars of Ravel's *Bolero*. The film was promoted as
an appreciation of gay male nudity from its posing-
pouch origins during the 1950s up to the hardcore
1970s. There are short clips of bodybuilder-turned-

109

actor Ed Fury, models posing for nudist magazines, clips from films which were never released, an oddity entitled "A Study of the Teenage Masturbation Syndrome", a montage of oral and glory hole scenes, a clip from *Gay Tarzan* and, rounding off the proceedings, clips from Halsted's *L. A. Plays Itself*, and *Boys in the Sand*.

Reviewing the film in *Variety*, Bruce King loathed every minute of it, and Halsted in particular:

> I question the film's contentions that it has presented the cream of the crop of gay movies. About Mr. Halstead, he is a drawback…with his nasal voice, giving a flat, vapid, insipid commentary. [16]

By the end of 1973, cracks were appearing in Casey's relationship with Tom Tryon, with his friends becoming increasingly worried about him as Tryon began showing his true colours now that the novelty of being enamoured with America's most illustrious gay porn star was starting to wear off. Tryon was so paranoid that his literary career would be affected should the world find out that he was gay, that he drank heavily. When drunk, which was often, he would turn violent and take his insecurities out of Casey by beating him, sometimes over some trifle. He frequently turned up at the theatre with bruises and aching ribs, and he is said never to have hit Tryon back. Because he was so terrified of this towering brute, Casey never lived with him, though they did stay at each other's apartments, and each time Tryon came to after one of his drunken bouts—weeping, apologetic, and swearing it would

110

never happen again, Casey believed him. Some of those closest to him actually believed that Tryon was schizophrenic, and so dangerous that he might one day go too far and end up killing their friend.

When *Tubstrip* was nearing the end of its run in Los Angeles, Tryon asked Casey to leave the show. He refused. His contract had been amended and extended—since Jim Cassidy's departure, the name Calvin Culver's was on the playbills above the title, and his name was on the star dressing-room door, a clear sign that *only* he was pulling in the crowds, while the rest of the cast was dispensable. Even so, he was getting weary of the long run. When the company arrived in San Francisco for a season, and there was talk of Jerry Douglas committing the show to the screen, he told one journalist at the after-show party, "*If* they do a film of *Tubstrip*, it ought to be an animated cartoon."

In January 1974, *Tubstrip* hit the tour circuit, with more than five-hundred performances with HOUSE FULL notices in every city. But if fans loved it, the reviews were frequently barbaric and homophobic. The first stop on the road was Boston, followed by Washington and Philadelphia, where *The Inquirer*'s William B. Collins observed of the premiere:

> Mixing the tender with the derisive, going for the easy laugh and the sentimental moment with arrant disregard of the niceties, the boys in this particular band are spending a night in a New York bath house, and their interest centers on the young attendant who they conclude has his own secret. Among the customers are a pair of S & M playmates

111

and two campy queens, one young and black and the other older and white. The older one [Wally] makes boy-boy porno and, as played by Jake Everett, frequently he is very funny as when he laments that "Linda Lovelace made four million, and *I* get arrested!" Like the quality of the material, the skill of the actors varies widely. Walter Holiday is all bitchy putdown as the black queen [Andy], who dons an Afro wig and really means business. **[17]**

Collins' unnamed colleague could not have been nastier when expressing his opinion of the play. Having been told over the phone by Jerry Douglas this was for a specialized audience, he concluded:

> We had in *The Boys in the Band* the pathos of homosexual society. Straight audiences could be moved by the plight of the twisted psyches that were so cleverly put on display. But a show like *Tubstrip* is something else, asserting as it does not the sickness but the validity of homosexual affection and homoerotic appeal. **[18]**

In Toronto, the show played a week at the Global Village Theatre. Herbert Whittaker, one of the country's most revered and feared critics observed:

> *Tubstrip*'s author, A.J. Kronengold, is after comedy and thrills. The latter are limited to male nudity frontal and backal. Its producers liken *Tubstrip* to the successful *The Boys in*

the Band. Nobody lifted an eyelid. Roughly speaking, this is the up-to-date answer to *Ladies Night in a Turkish Bath*, the '20s idea of a naughty show which today would seem redolent of lavender. **[19]**

The next stop on the road was Detroit, where *The Michigan Daily* ran an erroneous ad, "The First Gay Play Comes To Detroit...*Tubstrip*, A Homosexual Neil Simon Play". Jack Brake, the manager of the Leland House Hotel's Orleans Room, breached safety regulations by allowing patrons to stand in the aisles when all the seats sold in record time—he and they believing that this *was* a Simon play. No one asked for a refund, and this brought a scathing attack from the unnamed critic of the *Detroit Free Press*, who professed to loathing what he saw but nevertheless wrote about it at some length:

> What's a gay play called *Tubstrip* doing in a staid residential downtown hotel like the Leland House? *Tubstrip*? The show, a purported comedy about nine homosexuals in a steam bath, premiered Tuesday in the old-line Detroit hotel that has never hosted a *legitimate* play. The show's promoters insist it *is* a legitimate play about homosexuals, rather than a gay show-and-tell. They did not stress, however, that the show is engineered to catch a select audience, chiefly of homosexuals and the sexually curious. Asked what he thought of naked men performing in his elegant Orleans Room's Brake said, "There is only one nude

113

scene and it is in good taste. We are running *Tubstrip* for one week, with an optional return engagement. If there is ANY obscenity, they won't be back!" Later Brake said that the reported nude scene has been cut, and that *Tubstrip* will not play a return date. Nobody knows how the guests of the Leland will take to having *Tubstrip* downstairs in the big room off the main lobby....The first poster that hit the Leland lobby showed all. Almost immediately, strategic scraps of paper were pasted on the posters like fig leaves. The second wave of posters showed the young men topless, but trousered. These posters were removed too. **[20]**

In early April, the company arrived in Chicago for a six-weeks run at the Gill Community Arts Centre— where Casey was conspicuous by his absence at the premiere. Tom Tryon had this time *ordered* him to leave the show, and his refusal to do so had resulted in him getting a hiding which put him out of action for several days. And *still* he refused to give this brute his marching orders. He was replaced by his understudy, T.J. D'Angelo. Will Leonard of the *Chicago Tribune* was mocking and unimpressed:

> One nude homosexual says to another nude homosexual, "I was just thinking." And the second nude homosexual quips, "You'll try anything once, won't you?" And the gay lads in the audience break up in laughter. The above is a splendid example of the level

114

of the comedy. This is a campy and corny show, a deviate variation of Mae West's old parodies of sex....Indeed, this is a farce with no story, no brains, no character and no character development, no sense of direction. It's filled with "in" jokes that set off titters among the cognicenti in the audience, but it must be cheap-thrill pornography even to these experts. One A.J. Kronegold, billed as author, has brought together a variegated group apparently meant to represent a cross-section of the gay populace....They pose and prance and wave their genitals at one another, and pronounce their lines like characters in a kiddies' cartoon on TV, and only T.J. D'Agostino as Brian and Tom Van Stitzel as Richie seem to have much acting ability. [21]

A week into the run, Casey returned to the show, and the season was extended through until the end of May. He gave an interview for the next month's issue of *Viva, The International Magazine for Women* a mainstream magazine recently set up by porn baron Bob Guccione in direct competition with *Playgirl*. Other spreads in the publication included Warhol muse Joe Dallesandro, and hustler Eddie Bloom. Casey's fans had of course seen him naked before, perhaps not in a gym, but what surprised if not perturbed them was the editorial, under the heading, *The Naked Athlete*. For now, one imagines to please Tom Tryon—his friends believed that this was almost certainly the case—he was saying that he was *bi*sexual:

"It keeps me attractive to the opposite sex," says Cal Culver—explaining his continuing gymnasium exploits, even though he no longer needs to maintain the perfect physique of "Casey Donovan", in whose name Cal made his appearances in much more memorable classics of the gay cinema as *Boys in the Sand*, *The Back Row*, and *Casey.* "That part of my career is behind me now. It helped me bridge the gap into legitimate theatre and movies." Cal is able to make both sexes the object of his attention without any guilt. "I make love as the mood hits me, and if my mood is for a man, I'll find a man. Usually I go to the baths where you have the most freedom and anonymity to get into almost any gay or S & M scene. My kind of man is a dark muscular Italian or Mediterranean type, the construction worker type—almost exactly the opposite of what I prefer in a woman, which is a ballerina's body. [22]

He told Allan Leopold:

Everybody keeps saying how terrific my body is, but I never did anything with it until two years ago. When I made the Casey pictures, all I had done was cheerleading in college. Now I've started going to Gala Fitness an hour a day and working out on rings, trapeze and parallel bars, also some tumbling. I must be serious as I get up at eight and nine in the morning—two or three

116

days a week to do it. Right now I weigh 153 pounds and I augment my regimen with a lot of swimming and calisthenics. **[23]**

What Casey did not figure on was his mother buying a copy of *Viva* and seeing her son in all his naked glory—not only this, to read that he was not just a fashion model, but a major gay porn star, apparently the first time his parents had been made aware of this. He told Robert Richards of *Stallion*:

> *After that, she and my father were very anxious to move out of that town—they had no way of explaining that. My mom's dream is still that I'll make a G-rated movie she can show to the grandchildren.* **[24]**

Meanwhile, after a break of several weeks, *Tubstrip* headed for San Francisco, where it played a season at the Enterprise Theatre. Tom Tryon travelled with Casey, and rented a room in the same hotel as the rest of the company—the nearest they ever got to cohabiting. The I. Magnin department store hired him to do a fashion ad. This went well enough, until the *Chronicle*'s Herb Caen—known as "the voice and conscience of San Francisco—wrote in his column that the handsome young man in the tuxedo was "none other than the notorious porn star, Casey Donovan". Casey also met and was interviewed by Falcon Video's talent scout, Dennis Forbes, who observed in a newspaper column, "Cool Culver digs being hot Donovan, who gets off on taking friends to see himself on screen as Casey, doing what he does best—hand-dialogue."

117

By "hand-dialogue", Forbes was referring to the mock fisting scene with Val Martin in *Moving,* which Casey had acquired ahead of the film's release, and screened for friends in his dressing-room. Tom Tryon saw red, but managed to keep his temper under control—with Casey surrounded by enough muscular friends to protect him from those ever-ready fists.

On 29 October 1974, *Tubstrip* held the first of three previews at Broadway's Mayfair Theatre, and the premiere took place two evenings later. Mel Gussow may not have given it a favourable review in *The New York Times*, but the fact that one of America's most distinguished theatre critics mentioned it at all must have meant something to Jerry Douglas and the cast:

> The so-called comedy takes place in a homosexual bath house called "Boys Town". The cast includes an analyst who wears a leather harness and a snarl, an old queen who likes to be covered in Saran wrap (put him in the freezer immediately) and a masochist in a dog collar. The hero, who is the bath attendant, looks sullen....The dialogue is dreary....Actually the funniest line is, "I should never have come here tonight." Much of the acting is inept (the splashing is well-aimed). There is no sense of direction even in the evening's one chase. The stage is slippery and the play is as soggy as a wet towel. [25]

The *Oakland Tribune* was almost as scathing:

Over 500 performances during an 18-month tour into sundry crannies of the continent gives *Tubstrip* the dubious honour of being the first show with a nationwide gay housekeeping seal of approval....The much-traveled trifle settled down for a run at the just-off Broadway Mayfair Theatre on Halloween night. There were plenty of tricks but no treat for a straight intruder....The star is Calvin Culver, who does similar screen romps under the name Casey Donovan. The performers are enthusiastic and at least avoid excessive camp...."Have a good time," urged an usherette, one of the few females visible in the opening night throng of bare chests, satin shirts and leather jackets. Some other time, sister, somewhere else. [26]

The "somewhere else" was to be much further afield than New York, according to the notes in the Mayfair Theatre programme:

Many shows of the same genre have shied away from inviting critics. *Tubstrip* has found that even critics that don't like all of it have found it different and hilariously funny and entertaining. *Tubstrip* opens in London next February and has already been translated into French, German and Spanish. The movie version will be shot in New York in early April—a long history for a production that began in a 150-seat theatre that's now a parking lot.

119

Sadly, none of these productions—or the film— would see the light of day. *Tubstrip* took its final bow on 17 November 1974, after 25 performances (including the three previews), and Casey gave a huge sigh of relief. He had been approached by Radley Metzger once more and asked to appear in his new heterosexual hard-core blockbuster, *The Opening of Misty Beethoven*. Metzger had been assigned a high budget for this and had already booked the locations—New York, Rome and Paris, the latter inspiring him to direct under the pseudonym, Henry Paris. Casey had but one stipulation. He would appear in the film *only* as Casey Donovan—his way, he said, yet again, of bidding adieu to his porn moniker. Metzger agreed, though there would be no overseas travel for Casey, whose segment was shot in New York. This particular film would also be different—for the first time since *Eleanor*, he would be filmed having penetrative sex with a woman.

Tom Tryon.

Tubstrip, with Jim Cassidy.

The *Erotikus* premiere, August 1973.

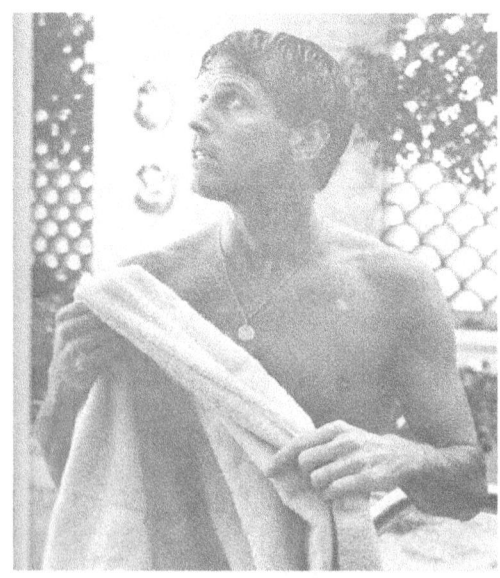

In his New York apartment, late 1973.

7: From *Misty* to *Aspen*

Casey was a sex-pig, hiding behind the face of a Botticelli cherub. (Jerry Douglas)

The Opening of Misty Beethoven was a porn take-off of George Bernard Shaw's *Pygmalion*. It tells the story of a sexologist who attempts to transform a lowly trollop—whose talent is limited mostly to masturbating old men dressed as Napoleon in sleazy Parisian cinemas—into "Goldenrod Girl", a classy lady of passion. Thus Henry Higgins becomes Dr Seymour Love, played bisexual porn legend Jamie Gillis, who had appeared in the original production of *Tubstrip*—while Eliza Doolittle becomes Dolores "Misty" Beethoven, played by Constance Money. Colonel Pickering becomes Geraldine Rich, played by Jacqueline Beudant. Towards the end of the film, Misty becomes convinced that she is never going to live up to Love's expectations, so he sets her the ultimate trial—his theory being that if she can have successful penetrative sex with a homosexual, then she is indeed worthy of the title "Goldenrod Girl".

Enter Jacques, a gay Geneva art dealer (Casey), though despite wearing make-up, he is not revealed as such until Misty has done with him and turned him straight! Casey is only on screen for seven minutes, but their scene is quite magical, and not as "full on" as the film's other sex scenes. He looks fetching in his white flares and flowing housecoat, open at the front to reveal his shaved chest. Wearing her favourite 'New Experience' perfume she arrives at Jacques' studio to be told that it is about to close. Geraldine, hiding in the shadows, flicks the switches in the fuse-box and causes a power-cut. She then puts Misty through her paces, rapping instructions through the ear-piece she is wearing, "Find an excuse to touch him. Say, 'Sir, you have something in your eye!' Move in on him! Run your tongue over his nipple! Lick the side of his cock!" They kiss passionately and a moment later he is naked, on the floor. "I'm gonna lick your cock like the inside of a ripe mango," she purrs, as she fellates him. Then she mounts and rides him—and not only does Casey produce the requisite money-shot, when he is done he penetrates Misty at once and climaxes a second time!

The Opening of Misty Beethoven won four AFAA Awards—Best Actor for Jamie Gillis, and Best Director, Scriptwriter and Editor for Randy Metzger. Tom Tryon is thought to have been slightly relieved that in this film, Casey had at least been filmed having straight sex, but he was still intent on persuading him to give up porn altogether. Casey, of course, would have been better giving *him* up, but as with many victims of domestic violence he was terrified of the consequences, should he end their relationship.

At the end of 1975, Casey auditioned for the part of Nicky in the Broadway play, *A Matter of Gravity*. Written by Enid Bagnold, as *Call Me Jacky*, this had premiered in Britain at the Oxford Playhouse in 1967, with Sybil Thorndike in the role of Mrs. Basil, an eccentric dowager who occupies just one room of her mansion, and whose life as a recluse is disrupted by the arrival of her grandson Nicky, four of his friends—and a new housekeeper, Dubois, who is able to levitate herself into the air. It is this that causes Mrs. Bagnold, a lifelong agnostic, to believe that God may really exist.

Directed by Noel Willman, and with Katharine Hepburn playing Mrs. Bagnold, the production was set to open on Broadway at the Broadhurst Theatre on 3 February 1976 for a fixed season—on account of Hepburn's busy schedule there would be eighty performances before it closed on 10 April. Another actor who auditioned for the part of Nicky was 23-year-old future *Superman* actor Christopher Reeve. Hepburn sat in on the sessions, and chose him. But if Casey did not get the part, he *did* get the man.

For Reeve, the opening night would prove a disaster. After delivering his opening line, allegedly because he had been so nervous that he had not eaten properly for days, he fainted on stage. On cue, Hepburn pronounced, as if this was a part of the scenario, "This boy's a goddam fool. He doesn't eat enough red meat!" His understudy then walked on, and finished the play for him.

Casey spoke of his two-month affair with Reeve to Robert Richards during a later in-depth interview with *Stallion*, but this was omitted from the feature for fear of litigation. He referred to him, without mentioning his name, in other interviews and wrote about him in his unpublished memoirs:

> *Christopher was a great lover, and I think I liberated him sexually. I didn't think he was gay, but he was willing to try anything once. He was curious...He was the man of my dreams.* [1]

125

The affair with Reeve ended a few days before *A Matter of Gravity* opened in New York—allegedly when Reeve made it clear that he did not want a porn star coming around to the dressing-room and exposing his secret. Nonplussed, Casey returned to Tom Tryon, who now affected a new approach to keep him under the thumb—employing him as editor for the book he was writing. His latest novel, *Lady*, had entered the best-sellers list and he had begun working on *Crowned Heads*, a quartet of novellas. These recount the story of a reclusive actress, Fedora, and her three co-stars in her 1955 film, *The Miracle of Santa Cristi*: fading leading man William Marsh, child star Bobbit—and a mentally ill dumb blonde named Lorna. All ended up hated by everyone in the profession, and are now forgotten. Tryon had submitted the synopsis to several publishers, and Alfred A. Knopf had offered him a lucrative contract—providing he could supply him with the completed manuscript within twelve weeks! Tryon dictated the story into a tape-recorder, and Casey typed it out—not only this, he made suggestions that might improve the storyline, which Tryon took on board. His acting career had been shunted to one side as his ebullient lover took control of his life. For three months Casey shunned his friends and society, arriving at Tryon's apartment at nine every morning, and not returning to his own—the only freedom he was granted—until after midnight.

There was an almighty bust-up with Tryon in April 1976, when *The Advocate* ran a piece announcing that Casey was planning on making his porn comeback:

The working title for the epic: *Masked Marvels*. The new film will be silent and episodic, in both colour and black and white, and will deal with fantasy sex for the everyday man. If he gets it off as planned, Donovan's finished product will offer porn-flick audiences a touch of class with a pinch of kink. A late summer release is hoped for. [2]

Casey was obviously thinking along the lines of a cross between *Boys in the Sand* and *The Back Row*. It would be an all-out "home" production—with him writing, directing, and of course performing. He had several co-stars in mind, including George Payne and Al Parker, more of whom later. Then, just as it looked like this was really going to happen, Tom Tryon put his foot down and the project was abandoned.

Crowned Heads was published in May 1976, and had earned Tryon a cool $4 million before the first copy rolled off the press. The rights were bought by Universal Studios for $1 million, though only the first novella, *Fedora*, made it to the screen, when the director was the legendary Billy Wilder, who wanted Marlene Dietrich to head the credits. She rejected the story as "too daft to laugh at", and Wilder subsequently signed her friend, the German actress Hildegard Knef. Supported were William Holden and Martha Keller.

Bearing in mind that Casey had a hand in it, the scenario is worthy of mention, albeit that Tryon did not have the decency to acknowledge his input. The comparisons with Garbo are only too obvious. After

127

decades at the top of her profession, Fedora retired to Crete, but while her co-stars have aged, her perfect features remained the same. Like Garbo in *Anna Karenina*, she committed suicide by throwing herself under a train, and amongst the mourners at her funeral is Hollywood producer and her former lover Barry Detweiler, who just weeks before had visited her in an attempt to talk her into making a remake of...*Anna Karenina*. Then, she told him that she was being held captive by a mysterious Polish countess, and the doctor responsible for keeping her looking so young. Then, at the funeral the countess reveals that *she* is Fedora, and that the woman who killed herself was her daughter, Antonia (Marthe Keller), who has been impersonating her for years.

While *Fedora* was in the pre-production stage, Tryon told Casey—one would imagine to keep him on side—that he would try and get him a part in the film, that of Antonia's film star lover. In fact, the British actor Michael York—playing himself—had already been assigned the role.

The final break from Tom Tryon occurred during the summer of 1977. It kicked off with an incident at New York's Uris Theatre in April, when Casey and Tryon attended a matinee performance of the musical, *Annie*. Tryon was accosted by an ex-lover who complimented him on his choice of "trick" for the afternoon. He stormed out of the theatre, all but dragging Casey with him. Within days, there were rumours that some sort of secret marriage had taken place. A few weeks later, Casey and Tryon spent the weekend at the New Hampton home of the playwright Edward Albee, and over dinner were shown a comment which Albee had circled in Rona

128

Barrett's gossip column in the *Hollywood Reporter*. Not naming names, the acid-tongued reporter had posed, "What male porn star is honeymooning on Long Island with an actor-turned-writer?"

Tryon left in the middle of the night. The next morning, finding an empty space next to him in the bed, Casey headed for Tryon's New York apartment to be told that he had taken a dawn flight to Los Angeles. They would never see each other again. Casey should have felt relieved to have finally been shot of this violent man. Instead, he was devastated and swore to friends that so long as he lived, he would never allow himself to fall in love again.

Casey's life had returned to normal, or as normal as he wanted it to be—no more restrictions on his social life, no one ordering him what to do, more crucially no one knocking him around. As a non-drinker he was not much of a bar/club person, but he did frequent the recently opened Studio 54—not to cruise for sex, but to mingle with the celebrities. Formerly the Gallo Opera House, this mecca for being seen was located at 254 West 54th Street, between Broadway and Manhattan. The regulars included Liza Minnelli, Mick Jagger, Elizabeth Taylor, Calvin Klein, Casey's friend Sylvia Miles, Lou Reed and John Travolta, to name but a few. Casey's favourite social activity was visiting the exclusively gay bath houses. Here there was no pretense. The men sitting around wrapped in towels, or more often wearing nothing at all, were here for one thing only—casual sex. It was all very private, if not above board, and as they were not cruising the streets, they were harming no one. It was only a few years later, with the start of the AIDS epidemic, that such behaviour was curtailed, mostly forcibly by the authorities. The stories that Tom Tryon came here or to Studio 54 looking for him, hoping to rekindle their affair, are unlikely to be true given Tryon's paranoia of anyone finding about his sexuality, even if this was one of the film and literary world's biggest open secrets.

Now that he was back in circulation other rumours started flying around. One stated that Casey had a fling with heterosexual porn star John Holmes, and another that he was involved with a "chubby blonde female". The latter may have been true—Casey had engaged in heterosexual sex on film, and had a female lover while shooting *Score* in Yugoslavia— but one finds it hard to believe that he would have wanted to get involved with a man like Holmes who was renowned for his homophobic stance.

Having been made aware of his literary talent by Tom Tryon, shortly after their split Casey began penning what was to have been his autobiography, but told as a novel and with name changes so as not to offend those who had crossed his path during his youth, and his transition from Calvin Culver to Casey Donovan. Bill Gross, the editor of Pocket Books, is believed to have paid him a substantial advance after reading a rough draft of the first two chapters. Casey's mistake was in telling a journalist about the project. Word got back to Tom Tryon who was convinced that, even with fictitious names, the intimate details of their relationship would be made public. Whether Tryon threatened him or paid him hush money is not known. Suffice to say the book was abandoned, and as such was a great loss to the gay communities of subsequent generations.

At the end of the year, he claimed just for fun, Casey placed an ad in *The Advocate*—advertising his services as an escort. The response was staggering, with many of those getting in touch curious as to whether this was *the* Casey Donovan, or an impostor attempting to cash in on his name.

Naturally there were a few cranks, but as a result of the ad—and another placed in the January issue —Casey amassed a coterie of clients, some of whom became lifelong friends. His fees ranged from $500 for one night, or $1,500 for the weekend, though he was not always interested in the money. Some of those he "serviced" *were* wealthy, flying him all over the world so that they were not having sex on their own doorstep, but many were not—just lonely or unattractive men whose only chance of finding love, albeit just for a night or a weekend, was near-impossible. In these special cases, Casey offered his services as a stud for free. Discretion was also essential. Many of these men were married or held positions of power, and would have been prejudiced against had their "secret" been revealed. Among his celebrity clients were fashion designer Versace, Paul Newman, and several A-list actors still living at the time of publication, and unable to be named for legal reasons. Casey is also said to have had several US senators on his list. Neither did the client have to be good-looking, as Jerry Douglas testified:

> *No matter how old, fat, bald, or grotesque a client was, he assured me, he could always find some one thing about the man to turn him on. I remember him saying, "If I like his*

eyes, for example, I can deal with the rest of it." He swore he had never had a client so physically unattractive that he could not get an erection, but he did confess that there had actually been one man so offensive that Cal refused to return for seconds. [3]

In the summer of 1978, Casey was contacted by Falcon Studios, and subsequently filmed what many critics and fans consider to have been his finest performance since *Boys in the Sand*. Founded by Chuck Holmes in 1971, Falcon Studios was and still is regarded as one of the most prestigious in gay pornography. One might say that any porn star from the 70s, 80s and 90s who did not work for Falcon at some stage during their career was not worthy of recognition. *The Other Side of Aspen* would be their first film to be sold to the public in all formats: Super 8, Regular 8—and most important of all, video. As such it would precipitate gay porn to a new and more accessible level. It was also one of the first productions to claim to have a soundtrack which was a part of the film, instead of being added later—frequently badly—by studio technicians.

Falcon's cameraman, Colin Meyer, suggested to Holmes and his production team that they would "make a killing" if they could persuade the three biggest gay stars of the day—Casey, Dick Fisk and Al Parker—to engage in an orgy which he was confident would set the gay porn world spinning. Fisk (Frank Fitts, 1955-83) had caused a sensation in Falcon's recently-released *Champs* and *Steam Heat*, and proved a pushover. Word had spread of how, since abandoning *Masked Marvels*, Casey had been "hungering" to work with Al Parker, but Falcon were not sure if Parker would be willing to appear with a man guaranteed of overshadowing him in every shot. He was in fact thrilled with the idea, and readily agreed. Likewise the director, Bill Clayton, was unsure that Casey would accept the part. He later said that, *had* he refused, the film would never have been made. And despite the title, only the exteriors were shot at Aspen, with all the interiors filmed over a three-day period at a woodland cabin at Lake Tahoe.

Parker (Andrew Okun, 1952-92) was one of the most important and most revered adult entertainers of his generation. Born in Natick, Massachusetts, when first arriving in California he had worked as a butler for *Playboy*'s Hugh Heffner. His career as a gay porn superstar began when he was "spotted" by Colt Studios, and given his famous name. His early loops were shot at his Hermosa Beach home. He achieved another kind of notoriety when he objected to having been circumcised as a baby, and enlisted with a foreskin restoration programme, resulting in the surgical procedure being performed by Dr. Ira Sharlip, a renowned urologist, and filmed for a television health documentary. Parker had shot two immensely successful loops for Falcon—*Weekend Lock-up* and *Rocks and Hard Places*. Whereas Casey was regarded as the sensitive type with the winning smile, ever-ready humour, and a twinkle in his eye, Parker was universally recognised as the ultimate macho-type, the one with the beard and lumberjack shirt which gay men all over America would copy. Like Casey he was sexually versatile— primarily a top but not averse to bottoming. Both he

133

and Fisk would die young—Parker of AIDS, aged forty, and Fisk in a car crash, at twenty-eight. The others in the film were Jeff Turk, Mike Flynn (in a non-sexual role), and Chad Benson, whose only film appearance this was—he and Fisk subsequently became lovers.

The Other Side of Aspen sees Casey and Parker acting off the cuff and requiring no directorial instruction. The opening scene had started off as a stills-photography session, but when it became clear that the actors could not control themselves, Colin Myer was instructed to start filming, in case the invaluable money-shots ended up being wasted. Inasmuch as they admired each other and constantly had sung each other's praises, Casey and Parker had never met, and declined to do so until the afternoon of the first shoot. Casey explained why:

> *I think it's easier because then you can perform on a strictly chemical level....I like the spontaneity of anonymous encounters. Al and I never met until the afternoon we flew from San Francisco to Lake Tahoe. A couple of hours later we did our first scene together and he wound up fisting me. Quite an experience!* [4]

Chuck Holmes recalled the ease with which the film had been made, and the fact that there had been no on-set histrionics, as often happened:

> *If you get the sexual energy going, the only thing that's holding you up is putting the film in the camera. You don't have to plan it, you hardly have to direct it. You merely have*

to capture it because it's happening right before your eyes as a natural sequence of sexual events. It doesn't always happen like that, but in this movie we had it because we had a 100% gay cast, 100% hot, and 100% hot for one another....There was nobody who said, "I'm a top only," or "Gee, I don't so this or I don't do that.". This movie was made at the height of the sexual revolution, and gay America was on the move. People were free and we had our rights for the first time, the idea that sex wasn't dirty and it didn't have to be dark and it didn't have to be hidden. And this [movie] *was the thing. I wanted to present sex in a really wholesome, athletic atmosphere.* **[5]**

Holmes intended *The Other Side of Aspen* to be a series of loops, but as shooting progressed he opted to link the scenes to form a storyline. As such it was promoted as Falcon's first full-length feature film—though at 35 minutes it cannot be deemed so. The company gaged its reception by mailing would-be customers and sales outlets *before* the editing process, and were stunned by the number of orders that came in, enabling the video to sell more copies than any other gay porn film to date. Writer, activist and media strategist Jeffrey Escoffier observed:

The Other Side of Aspen was Falcon's first blockbuster, and like all blockbusters it accounted for the lion's share of Falcon's earnings. It's explosive impact marked a turning point for a company selling its films

135

only through mail-order transactions—unwittingly preparing it for the coming age of the VCR. The success of *Aspen* transformed Falcon into a different sort of company—one that began to increase its production values and adopt other policies such as signing performers as exclusives—that made it into the powerhouse of gay porn companies. With *Aspen*, Falcon discovered the Midas formula. [6]

The scenario is confusing. In the sound version the actors speak when speech would not be possible—when mouths are otherwise occupied—and the rest of the time without moving their lips, making it obvious that their lines have been added at the editing stage, in Casey's case using someone else's voice. There is none of the finesse of his earlier work. All the viewer gets is half an hour of interrupted raw sex, with Casey getting lost in the middle of it. The five *Aspen* sequels are all better, though none of their actors are as well-endowed as here. The doyenne of gay porn sites, *The Gay Erotic Video Index*, did not know what to make of it:

> The silent version needs at least two screenings before it begins to make much sense. On the first screening it was not at all clear that the jogger and the skier are the same guy, for example, and the periodic scene changes to the apartment in San Francisco weren't at all clear until the entire complex of the story was established, and remembered.

The story, such as it is, begins with ski instructor Jeff Turk leaving his San Francisco apartment and going out for a jog while waiting for his lover, Mike Flynn, to show up. The camera follows him through the streets as he mumbles almost incoherently about an incident that happened two months ago on the slopes at Aspen. Cut to the scene at the snowbound cabin, where he arrives to give lessons to Dick Fisk and Chad Benson, but instead watches them through the window while they are having sex. The camera returns to Jeff, telling a more of his story, and then goes back to the couple in the cabin. When they are done, we see Jeff and Mike in their apartment and Jeff resuming his tale, his voice abruptly changing to someone else's halfway through. He recalls what he saw through another window—Casey, aka the power bottom sex-slave, engaged in rough sex with Al Parker, while Dick emerges from the shower to make up a threesome. Jeff adds how he revealed himself and joined the group, from which point the running commentary from the four—with "Ah-ha!" pronounced over fifty times—becomes increasingly annoying. Finally, Chad joins in and, filmed looking down on the action from the upstairs balcony, they gang-bang Casey. The film ends with Jeff and Mike in bed at the apartment. All this reminiscing has made him feel horny, he says, and just before the credits roll it becomes obvious that they are going to have sex, though we do not get to see this—a pity, for an extra fifteen minutes with these two very engaging men would have made the production that much better, and given fans that much more value for money.

137

Casey called Christopher Reeve,
"The man of my dreams."

With Al Parker in *The Other Side of Aspen*.

8: Florida Calling!

I don't do drugs, though I experimented a little at the time. I don't smoke or drink alcohol. I'm trying to keep it together. I know about forty people who have died in the past two years. Without drugging or drinking, I'm keeping healthy. (Casey)

As had happened after completing *The Back Row*, Casey started having doubts about the new film, asking himself if he had gone *too* far. The former had also concluded with a gang bang scene, but it had contained a storyline which many gay men identified with—the risks of picking up a stranger who might not have been all that he seemed. It had contained passion, romance, cynical humour—and a great deal of fantasising between the protagonists. *Aspen* had none of this, just sex for sex sake.

Once again, Casey considered giving up porn and concentrating on his legitimate acting career as Calvin Culver. He had turned thirty-five during the production of *Aspen*, and wanted to get out of the "meat market" before risking making himself look ridiculous, as Val Martin had in *Moving*.

Salvation for now came at the end of 1978 when Casey relocated to Key West, Florida. The resort was one of the first in America to openly court gay tourists. It also boasted its quota of celebrity residents: President Truman, and writers Tennessee Williams, Truman Capote and Ernest Hemingway all lived here, or were regular visitors. Since placing the ad in *The Advocate* it had been Casey's dream to own his own home. The rent on his New York apartment had risen to $600 per month, which he looked upon as throwing his money down the drain. Florida, he decided, was where he needed to be. Using some of money he had saved from his hustling fees, he put down a substantial deposit on 617 Whitehead, a two-storey, nine-roomed property with a pool, built in 1948, not far from the Hemingway Museum. He brought in a team of renovators, converted the outbuildings into holiday chalets, and Casa Donovan was born.

Some of the reports in the years after his death over what supposedly transpired at Casey's new home, usually during his absence—and the general running of the place—were not only untrue, but offensive towards his memory. As with "lovers" recalling their sexual exploits—using fake aliases and grossly exaggerated if not made up entirely— these stories should be taken with a liberal dose of salt. Casey was *not* the proprietor of a run-down shack which he had turned into a brothel. Drugs and sex parties were *not* the order of the day, otherwise the other property owners on Whitehead would have complained to the authorities. Casa Donovan was an ordinary, respectable and affordable men-only guest house. Casey did *not* have to hustle to meet keep the place afloat. Therefore it is not my intention to put him down, as others ungallantly have, for trying.

Soon after his arrival in Florida, Casey learned that Victor Nunez, a local independent film maker, was casting for the screen version of Marjorie Kinnan Rawlings' 1932 short story, *Gal Young Un*. Set in 1930 during the Prohibition era, this tells of a middle-aged spinster, Mattie Siles, who is charmed

141

into marrying Trax, an opportunist bootlegger twenty years her junior. To play Mattie, Nunez hired local English professor Dana Preu, herself widowed and with no acting experience whatsoever. Though she exonerates herself extremely well here, she only made one more film before retiring to care for her elderly mother. David Peck, who played Trax, was also a newcomer. It would take another twenty years to tempt him back to the screen after this one, and then there would be just two more films. Casey played Trax's hired hand, Jeb Lantry. What is interesting is that Nunez refused to sign him as Calvin Culver, and he appears in the credits as Casey Donovan. Shot on a budget of $94,000, the film was part-financed by the National Endowment for the Arts and the Florida Fine Arts Council, and had a gross revenue of $500.000.

Shot on location not far from Casey's new home, *Gal Young Un* opens with Mattie smoking her pipe and content with living a frugal existence in the pinewoods with just her cat for company. When cocky Trax (David Peck) arrives in town and learns that she has been bequeathed a fortune by her father, he woos and marries her. She finances his moonshining operation and they hire Jed Langtry— who in one scene Mattie addresses as Cal!—and his brother (Mike Garlington) to construct a whisky still. It is not long, however, before Trax reveals his sadistic side. From his illegal earnings he buys an expensive Packard, which he drives to town to visit the speakeasy and pick up women. When he brings one of these home—the "gal young un" of the film's title—and soon starts treating her the way he has Mattie the two women bond, Mattie destroys the still and sets Trax's car on fire, and the creep is sent along his way, back to wherever he came from.

The film premiered on 24 September 1979 at the New York Film Festival, and was singled out by *The New York Times* as, "An astonishingly good first feature." *The New Statesman* hailed it "a gem of a film". The following month it was screened at the Chicago International Festival where it won the Silver Hugo Award for Best First Feature. It later won top prize at the USA Film & Video Festival, and the O. Henry Award. *The New Statesman* hailed it "a gem of a film".

It was a return to the "norm", when just weeks after finishing *Gal Young Un*, Casey was contacted by Tim Kinkaid and Sam Christensen, who as "brothers" Joe and Sam Gage were responsible for *The Working Man Trilogy*, the most successful gay porn series of the pre-condom age. Photographed by Richard Youngblood, this road movies saga featured a new breed of porn star, as personified by Al Parker in *The Other Side of Aspen*: working class types who were hyper-butch, hirsute, usually with beards or moustaches or both, and who refused to be categorized as tops or bottoms, preferring always to be sexually versatile. Other Gage specialities were flashbacks and voyeurism. Many critics have said that their only fault was not always using the actors' own voices when overdubbing the dialogue—it is believed because some of these spoke effeminately, and would therefore have detracted from the overall macho effect. Jerry Douglas, who considered the films extensions of what he had achieved in the closing scene of *The Back Row*, observed of the trilogy:

143

It introduced a new sort of hero to the gay film, and celebrated the freedom of the sexual revolution that had spread across America during the years that they were being made. Today, in retrospect, the trio stand together as the definitive cinematic statement on the emergence of the macho homosexual whose sexual transiency and voracity influenced larger and larger numbers of gay men—until the advent of AIDS. [1]

Joe Gage said he preferred shooting masturbation scenes to penetration scenes, and thus kept the latter down to a minimum:

The whole idea of making homosexual pornography is the worship of the phallus, the worship of the penis. If you're going to make homosexual pornography, you'd better light the dick....You're highlighting the penis. That's what it's all about. [2]

The character common to all three films is Hank (Richard Locke, 1941-96), a bearded, unattractive trucker who in the first film, *Kansas City Trucker Show*, released in 1976, is assigned to "straight" boy Steven Boyd, who becomes the object of his desire. Before setting off on their first haul, Hank and his boss—the legendary Jack Wrangler—have sex. Henceforth, at every stop on the road beefy Hank encounters equally unattractive hairy types with moustaches and/or beards who masturbate or have sex in flashbacks, flashbacks within flashbacks, and

144

dream sequences where all sense of reality is abandoned. Watching this today, one wonders what all the fuss was about. There is no real storyline, not one scene is acted out in full, and the final fifteen minutes of the film is a senseless mish-mash of anonymous sex, with darkened extreme close-ups of men ejaculating to an excruciatingly noisy musical soundtrack.

The second film in the trilogy, *El Paso Wrecking Corp*, is of such unbelievably dire quality that one is hard put to see, let alone care what is happening on the screen for much of the time. Hank and buddy Gene (Fred Halsted) are fired from their trucker jobs after getting drunk and brawling. Hailed by one critic as "the gay man's Peter Fonda and Dennis Hopper" (from *Easy Rider*), they hit the road in search of blue-collar work and head for El Paso, and naturally have lots of rough sex at every stop along the way. Like its predecessor, the lengthy glory-hole scene with its blurred, non-stop ejaculation shots instinctively has one reaching for the fast-forward button. One may only wonder why a star as eclectic as Halsted (1941-89) should have wished to add his name to such amateurish trash.

The final film in the trilogy, *L. A. Tool & Die*, was a distinct improvement, and in parts even borders on the romantic. The Gage brothers explore serious topics such as grieving (via a flashback death scene) and the Vietnam War. Hank, looking less unkempt than in the previous two films, finds the love of his life, Wylie (Will Seagers) at the beginning of the story, but lets him go and spends the rest of his on-screen time searching for him, engaging in sleazy orgies along the way.   The supports also are better-

145

known: besides Casey there is Derrick Stanton, Paul Baressi, Michael Kearns (who had worked with Casey in *Tubstrip*), and Bob Blount—a stunning bearded blond who had appeared as the centerfold in the April 1979 issue of *Playgirl*. There is humour when film director Paul Barresi stops his car to have sex with his girlfriend in an outdoor open urinal. When they are done, he flings his condom at the young backpacker (Shawn Victors) who has been perving on them from the bushes. The film ends with Hank finally getting his man and settling down with him. This closing scene, where they discover water in the plot of land Hank has bought, was inspired by a similar scene in *Come to the Stable*— in which Loretta Young played a nun!

The scene featuring Casey has nothing to do with the rest of the story, and appears at various stages of the film, depending on the print. He plays Fred, who is driving along a country road at night when a girl (Terri Hannon) flags him down and asks for a lift. The sympathetic hero obliges, and the next thing she is pulling a gun on him, ordering him out of the car, and handcuffing him to a tree. We then see the lower half of a man creeping through the trees, and a moment later he has ripped Fred's clothes off and is sodomizing him. We soon realize that all is not what is seems when Fred's expression changes from pretend fear to abject ecstasy—what we have just witnessed is a case of role-playing by the trio, for the stranger (Derrick Stanton) is Fred's lover. Thus as the girl drives off, the men head home, their lust assuaged for now.

There was a tragic coda to the production, when in September 1979, just weeks after shooting wrapped,

146

Bob Blount was killed in a motorcycle accident. He was just thirty-one, and Casey was devastated. It had been his intention for them to work together in his next film, whatever this might have been.

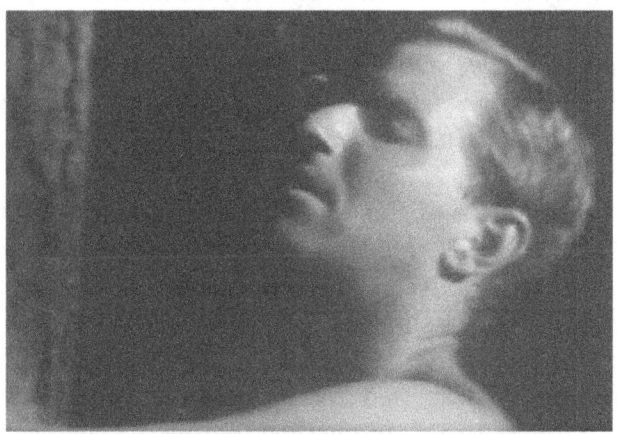

In the gloom, Fred (Casey) gets his "come-uppance" in *L. A. Tool & Die*!

147

9: Faraway Places

After my sixth tour with gay men under the auspices of Hanns Ebensten, I am still awed and proud by so many diverse men who seem to form a bond of goodwill and adventure so quickly without jealousy or pretence. (Casey)

Little is known of Casey's visit to Britain during the autumn of 1980. He was a guest of the Edinburgh Festival in August, when *Gal Young Un* was one of the highlights—similarly when it was screened at the London Film Festival on 24 November. The trip certainly reawakened the wanderlust in him, for when he returned home just before Christmas he began preparing for a new aspect of his career—that of "speciality" tour guide!

In Miami, Casey had been organizing day-tours for a while—escorting primarily gay tourists around the city, visiting the Hemingway Museum and such. Now, he opted to branch out and accepted a position with Star Tours Inc., a Hollywood-based company which offered well-heeled patrons the opportunity to travel overseas, each tour accompanied by a celebrity guide. His first commission, in the autumn of 1981, was escorting a group of gay businessmen of varying ages to Italy—firstly to Milan, then on to Florence, Venice and Rome, the cities he had taken in during his hustling jaunt in the early 1970s. In their promotional material, Star Tours Inc. used one of the Roy Blakey photographs that had appeared on the cover of *After Dark*, and the caption, "Mister

148

Personality Plus Himself—Superstar Casey Donovan!"

Some of the stories that sprang up about Casey's escapades during the trip were fictitious, involving supposed adventures which would never have been tolerated by the Italian authorities. Rumours that he organized outings for his "clients" to meet men and have sex in tourist hotspots—such as actually *inside* the Vatican and the Coliseum—were nonsensical exercises in wishful thinking. Again, as with those concocted about his exploits at his parents' trailer park, and what happened in the dressing-room after his theatrical performances, it was as if these people *had* to boast that it was not possible to spend time in Casey's company without sex being involved.

One of the guests at Casa Donovan, when Casey returned from Italy, was Val Martin, his co-star in *Moving*. Martin and another porn star, Richard Trask, had also recently jumped on the "tour guide bandwagon", and signed up with Hanns Ebensten (1923-2006), the crème de la crème of gay travel specialists. Born in Germany, Ebensten had escaped the holocaust and served in the British Army during World War II—hence his cut-glass English accent. He had moved to America and settled in Key West around 1970, and early in 1972 he and his long term partner, Brian Kenney, had led their first group of gay tourists on a rafting trip down the Grand Canyon. His business would thrive with him at the helm for another thirty years (it is still going strong today), and he would pen travelogues covering his adventures, the best-known being *Volleyball with the Cuna Indians*. Some years later he recalled what had led to them setting up their business:

149

Why do gay men have a special affinity for travelling together? The company! Why would you want to sit on a motor coach next to a little lady who points out the window and says, "Look at that lovely little girl selling oranges!" when you can sit next to a man who points out the window and says, "Look at the package on that guy!" [1]

When Casey learned that Ebensten lived within walking distance of Casa Donovan, he went to see him, explained about the recent trip to Italy, and asked if he might have a job as a celebrity tour guide on a trial basis. Ebensten had hired Martin and Trask as a gimmick, hoping that doing so would attract more gay clients if they were to be escorted around by someone moderately famous. Then when these two had left his employ and no more Colt models had been available, and when this had not affected his business, Ebensten had decided just to offer his clients what they really wanted—fulfilling trips around the world, tailored to suit discerning gay men, to destinations not then always offered by other travel companies—such far-off climes as Easter Island, Egypt, and the Amazon. Ebensten was not sure that he wanted a man on board who was not just a porn star, but a hustler! Casey offered a "compromise": he would travel with Ebensten on his next trip—as a paying guest—and allow him to decide for himself whether or not he was worthy of employment. Doubtless he was taken aback when Ebensten changed his mind and took him on, on a trial basis—and then informed him that the next trip would see them spending two weeks in China!

150

The company set off in May 1982 and Ebensten, who appears never to have watched any of Casey's films, was at once bowled over by his charm:

> *This, the most famous—or notorious—gay sex symbol of the time was, surprisingly, a highly educated, enormously well-read and considerate man with impeccable manners who dressed in a most conservative style. Good-looking but in no way either pretty or aggressively handsome, with a teenager's slim and graceful figure that he had maintained for over twenty years, he was the sort of man with whom one could be seen anywhere and whom one could unhesitatingly introduce to one's mother.* [2]

Before setting off on the trip, Casey read up on China: the country's culture, politics and religion, and its culinary tastes which Ebensten said he found disgusting. In his book he explains that while Casey carried just one small duffel bag, he rarely saw him wearing the same clothes twice—and that he was equally at home mixing with the locals, or dining with the governor of Anhui Province. He recalls an episode when a Chinese woman came up to Casey and, having heard that he was a movie star, asked him to describe a film that he had been in. His response was that his favourite (*Boys in the Sand*) had been about a group of friends who had gone to an island resort for the summer, to deal with the complications of their relationships!

Ebensten recalled the group's visit to the Huang Shan Mountains and of how disappointing the Great

151

Wall had been—but of how Casey's antics at the Summer Palace, near Beijing. had everyone in stitches. In the throne-room here, female visitors were allowed to pose and be photographed in court robes dating from the reign of Empress Dowager Cixi, at the end of the 19th century. Casey asked the curator if *he* and his fellow travelers might possibly pose in these, while Ebensten agreed to foot the bill:

> *In a moment of inspiration I told all the tour members to select gowns and headdresses, and my "discerning gentlemen" accepted the offer with alacrity and began to pull the heavily embroidered, flowered, bejeweled gowns from their hangers, snatched them out of one another's hands, put them on, discarded them for other, even more elaborate and gaudy robes, selected the most magnificent and largest diadems, enormous hats with feathers and bells and pom-poms, headdresses with glittering stones of paste and cut-glass ornaments like chandeliers, with silk fringes hanging seductively over their faces. The women attendants were frantic.* [3]

And of course, Casey had passed his test. Halfway through the trip, Ebensten offered him a permanent, highly-paid position—which over the next five years would see him travelling the world, visiting locations he had only ever dreamed of seeing: the Galapagos Islands, Egypt, the Canadian Rockies, Peru, India, Nepal and Australia. Ebensten concluded:

I realized that he possessed to a high degree the qualities that are essential for a tour leader: meticulous attention to detail; the patience of an angel; the ability to charm not only his fellow travelers but also airline, railroad, ship, and hotel staff and overzealous officials, and to turn a potentially troublesome situation into an unexpected, interesting travel experience. [4]

Again, there were rumours that Casey took advantage of these trips to turn tricks overseas, and that he arranged sexual encounters for his fellow travelers—which would *not* have been tolerated by Ebensten, or the strict and often homophobic authorities of some of the countries they visited. He did not however deny that bonding took place among the travelers themselves—as might have happened with any other tour group—gay or straight, during a trip to the Grand Canyon:

It was interesting that a certain amount of pair-bonding developed by the second night's camp. I'm not sure of the amount of sexual activity that transpired over nine days but I think the shared private campsites came out of the joy of lying naked next to a kindred spirit in the heated air along a roaring river, gazing up at billions of galaxies, counting shooting stars. Watching the moon becoming fuller night after night, and discussing the day's events, life's hopes, past experiences and dreams. I think each of us discovered a lot of things about ourselves on this expedition. Most of us found hidden physical strengths we didn't know we had or hadn't used in a long time. There were strengths of compassion and tolerance. And there were strengths of daring and character that each man summoned out of those dark recesses that are sometimes hidden in our city lives. [5]

One encounter which *did* take place on one trip, and which was very definitely non-sexual, was recalled by Ebensten:

Because he knew many members of the bon ton*, he was able to enhance the pleasures of those who toured with him by chance encounters. During a tour to the Carnival in Venice, when he led the group into Harry's Bar, a distinguished Italian prince arose from his banquette and called out, "Calvino, mio caro! What a surprise"—and promptly invited him and his tour members to afternoon tea next day in his palazzo.* [6]

When he returned to Miami, Casey received a call from Joe Gage, who offered him the part of Marty King in his next production, *Heatstroke*. In the film, the main protagonist, Rory (Roy Garrett) provides the narration, while Casey/Marty—the credits state that he appears "by special arrangement with Casa Donovan"—provides the voice-over linking the scenes. On a ranch in Montana, the workers are bullied and persistently humiliated by their heartless foreman, Shep (Locke), who gives every impression of being straight. So too does the protagonist, Rory (Roy Garrett), who with the other ranch hands heads for town where a rodeo is taking place, and visits a peep show where he ends up performing oral sex on a woman. When two other men watching her begin masturbating, this excites his curiosity, hitherto suppressed. Soon afterwards he has gay sex for the first time, an experience he finds frightening because the other man is so dominant, and thinks that his power over him makes him the superior partner, inasmuch as Shep thinks he is better than the other ranch hands. Therefore he hatches a plot to exact his revenge on Shep—hence the film's tagline, "Male Bonding...With A Vengeance!" Before this happens, Shep himself needs to settle a score when he is visited by former marine Pete (Clay Russell), who was once married to Shep's wife. After discussing their marital problems with the same woman, and after some initial reluctance on Shep's part, the two engage in oral sex while the camera cuts into the scene with footage of the rodeo. Back on the farm we see Jud (Clinton Coe), who has eschewed going to the rodeo to stay home—to read Rollo May's psychological study, *Love and Will*. Taking a break from this, he goes for a walk in the woods and we hear Casey pronounce, "The *best* homo sex is impersonal, promiscuous, anonymous, public!" before reciting *Jud's Fantasy*, a poem by Rick L. Pollack, who scripted the film. Then we see him as Marty, looking stunning with a five o'clock shadow and engaged in fellating a faceless black man while Jud masturbates—until he joins in with Casey performing oral sex with several

155

others who arrive on the scene. Following this extravaganza is a scene where John Steele is refused admittance to a sex club because he is "over the hill"—no problem, as he soon hooks up with another rejectee, "too preppy" Bud Wallace, for a hot session around the back of the building! On and on it goes, until the stupendous finale orgy where all the ranch hands—along with Casey, John Steele and Clay Russell—pitch in, and formerly timid Rory exacts his revenge on the once-bullying Shep...by topping him!

Next it was from Cage to Rage. Christopher Rage (1948-91) was an all-rounder: porn star, model, director and singer. His videos were extreme, with titles such as *Three Little Pigs*, *Toilets* and *Tramps* giving viewers what it said on the box: sweaty sex with often unattractive men in dirty locations, filthy talk, leather, sex toys, scat and water sports. Rage signed Casey to appear in two films—*Sleaze*, and *Christopher Rage's Best of the Superstars*. Both featured the biggest name on his books: Scorpio who, like Al Parker, Casey had wanted to work with for some time.

Scorpio (Wilbur Weiss, 1952-98) was so-named because of his zodiac sign—his birthday was 1 November, one day before Casey's. A stunning, beefy blonde with tousled hair, like Casey he had grown up in a trailer park. He had started out as a dancer-stripper in his native New Jersey, with his gay-friendly mother Mildred making his costumes, and filmed his first loop, *Double Scorpio*, in 1978, an oddity where he is in a porn theatre watching himself masturbating on the screen, before getting up and going to the screen to have sex with himself.

156

He is known to have been extremely difficult on the set, to such an extent that few actors wanted to have anything to do with him once they had suffered the brunt of his unpredictable temper. In his time he particularly made enemies of Jack Wrangler, and George Payne, his co-star in *Centurions of Rome*. He hated gay-for-pay actors, telling one magazine, "I'd rather work with a completely gay cast instead of straights. I don't like straight people in a gay film. I want someone that's going to reciprocate. I don't need a 'do-me queen.'"

Casey, on the other hand, Scorpio placed on a pedestal, later saying that he was the best actor he had *ever* worked with. Christopher Rage did not however partner them in *Sleaze*, promoted as a showcase for Scorpio, even though Casey's name headed the credits. In the first scene, he partnered him with himself, in the second with David Stoner, and in the closing scene again with himself, Roberto Castro—and Daniel Holt, Rage's other major name with whom Casey performs his one scene in the film. Swiss-born Holt (Daniel Niedorf) (1958-93) was a rare commodity in gay porn in that he always sold himself short and refused to allow his name to head the credits, even when he was the star of the film—his theory being that whoever he appeared with was a far better performer than he was. Like Scorpio, he was not easy to get along with, and as he progressed through his career became increasingly dependent on the drugs which led to his fatal overdose when he was just thirty-five.

Casey's scene with Daniel Holt, later included in Rage's *Sex Toilets* compilation, sees him—dressed immaculately in suit, shirt and tie—stumbling into a dirty mensroom, where he gets more than he bargained for from Daniel, looking very wholesome in his plaid shirt. In some prints of the film, there is a final scene where Casey, Holt and David Stoner have sex in a hot-tub. But if the viewer was expecting to watch a series of romantic episodes, the publicity blurb gave it to him straight:

> It ain't no love story. Chris Rage serves up a shocking tale of men who meet in an abandoned building on 42nd Street for savage, fantasy filled sex. There's the cowboy room, the parachute room, the hot tub room—and the room of forbidden pleasures. You'll want to enter them all! [7]

Skinflicks observed of the film and its decidedly offbeat soundtrack:

> At first it's extremely difficult to understand what's being said: the distortion is too great....At the conclusion of the shot, bits of sexual dialogue come out clearly: Casey Donovan saying, "You want to fuck my ass? You like that ass?" distorted to the point where the effect is as eerie as it is sexual. We're given a cold, creative vantage point, not knowing how to gauge the reality of the moment, having to find a way to make it work by engaging actively with the material.

In *Best of the Superstars*, Casey and Scorpio kick off the action and are in their element, as they wake up next to each other, while the morning sun streaks

158

through the blinds. Casey had just turned thirty-eight, but with a shorter hair style looks ten years younger as he dominates throughout a lengthy, sweaty turn-and-turn-about penetration scenario. Throughout the action, he talks dirty for the first time in a film, a running commentary which is more hilariously amusing than shocking—sweat dripping off his chin he drawls in a voice half an octave lower than usual to a mesmerized Scorpio, "Beautiful, baby. Beautiful fucking load right on your fucking tits!" Then in the next scene George Payne, Casey's co-star from *The Back Row*, fascinates in a rough-and-ready, surreal sequence—billed as "a sizzling psychodrama"—with John Wilson and Lee Martin. Christopher Rage said afterwards that these two were the best scenes he had ever filmed. Therefore what follows is dull by comparison—including solos from Richard Locke and Rage himself, and a three-way between Locke, Scorpio and, in his only porn outing, Scorpio's then lover Philip Demato.

159

Casey with Scorpio.

Casey Donovan, tour guide extraordinaire!

10: Always Ready!

Even in his later films, as he aged and his onscreen sexual escapades became harder core, he maintained an impenetrable innocence. He never appeared jaded or tired. The Image prevailed. (Michael Kearns)

Casey added yet another string to his bow—that of agony aunt—when Jerry Douglas, now the editor of *Stallion*, commissioned him to write a monthly column. *Letters to Casey* would run until May 1987. He told Rob Richards of *Manshots*:

> *For years I'd been receiving fan letters with questions the writers couldn't seem to ask of anyone else. With me, they felt comfortable.*
> *So, when Jerry Douglas,* Stallion's *editor, approached me to do an Ann Landers-type column, it seemed a natural. I could see that I might be able to help some men become happy homosexuals, and as it's turned out, it's been wonderful for me. It's given me the opportunity to actually sit down and write and gear myself to do my own autobiography.* [1]

This would *not* be a conventional autobiography:

> *I'm planning to do my own book as a serious self-analysis—it's going to be by both Casey Donovan and Cal Culver. I want to do it as*

an interview between my two personas—
getting into both my minds, so to speak—to
explore both the wholesome corn-fed boy
and that other person who does all that wild
fuck-stuff on film. [2]

Jerry Douglas remembered:

Cal was as sexually driven as any individual
I've ever known. He would appear at my
Stallion *office to drop off his column,*
usually about noon, and with a giggle, try
and determine how he could go to the baths,
service at least one client (and usually
more), attend the theatre, and hit the Central
Park rambles before retiring for the night.
He liked to joke that, like Dorian Gray, he
would hate to see the portrait in his attic,
but his column was always on time, he was
unfailingly responsible, and he always,
somehow, looked sensational whenever the
camera was about to roll or an audience
about to assemble. He was at once the most
disciplined and undisciplined human being
I've ever known, a maelstrom of paradoxes
and demons beneath a façade of absolute
normality. [3]

In his column, Casey dealt frankly and eloquently
with all kinds of problems experienced by the gay
community: how to come out to one's parents,
exercise routines, dietary advice, and how to get the
best out of one's sex life. His own was not as hectic
as it once had been. Though, at almost forty, he was

still a very attractive man, he *was* hustling less and had begun taking notice of the new "plague" that had begun affecting gay men, mostly in big cities such as New York and San Francisco. As such he advised his readers to slow down with their intake of sexual partners. Some criticized him for being hypocritical: the fact that he was telling people not to have as much sex, while he was getting more rampant and dirtier on the screen. They were of course missing the point, the one stressed by Chi Chi LaRue, one of the greatest porn directors of all time who would make a point of stressing to the next, AIDS-aware generation:

> *Sex is a wonderful and natural thing, and it's beautiful, not dirty or sinful or wrong. Most Christians are way off base about that. What I provide with my movies is an outlet for that wonderful, miraculous creation. If people can stay at home and jerk off to one of my films, rather than going to the clubs or the baths and having unsafe sex with some stranger of uncertain morals and dubious hygiene, then I'm helping to keep them healthy and safe and alive. It's an alternative to safe sex.* **[4]**

AIDS was very much in its infancy so far as public knowledge of the disease was concerned—indeed, though the AIDS epidemic officially began in June 1981, when the U.S. Centers for Disease Control &

Prevention first reported the symptoms in five gay men in Los Angeles—the term was little used. The medical profession had no idea what caused it, let alone how to prevent it, other than to suggest to gay men—as Casey had in his column—to cut down on the number of sexual partners. In heterosexual porn, performers rarely used condoms, and in gay films never. The only fear actors had until now was the risk of venereal diseases, most of which were dealt with by way of a visit to an STD clinic. Gay porn stars were putting themselves at risk—around sixty per cent of Casey's generation of gay porn stars succumbed to the disease over the next decade—while having no idea that they *were* taking risks. It is believed that the first gay porn star to die of AIDS was Wade Nichols, in January 1985.

Casey cautiously touched on the subject in a later interview for *Stallion*, in an issue promoting *AIDS: The Mystery & the Solution*, one of the first studies of the disease by Alan Cantwell, M.D. In this, at a time when ignorance ruled, Cantwell came up with a conspiracy theory that the disease may have been a biological warfare virus added to a hepatitis B vaccine to target American homosexuals. When asked by Robert Richards what most worried the readers of his column, Casey replied:

> *It never changes. It's the classic gay problem. "Where and how do I find a lover?" It seems especially urgent now that*

so many are nervous about going to bars and baths. The majority of gay men seem to feel desperately that they must have a lover and, of course, meeting someone is more difficult with the serious health problems and the wave of anti-promiscuity we're facing. **[5]**

Regarding this promiscuity among the non-closeted members of the gay community he added:

I suppose most people are programmed to mate, like all animals—but the chemistry is so different in male-male relationships than it is in male-female liaisons. I'm not sure one-on-one relationships are possible between men. **[6]**

Casey spoke of his relationship with Tom Tryon, though Richards was asked not to divulge his name:

During my second [long] *relationship, I began to feel I was being taken advantage of, that I was being taken for granted and not getting enough emotional feedback. Today, I'm not so sure I could have a lover again. I'm not looking, and of course, that's the surefire way to find one, but I'm not sure I want to live in a house in the country with someone when I'm sixty. I think I may want to live in a house in the country—but alone!*

166

Living in New York I hardly ever feel lonesome, there's so much human contact here. I can hardly walk to the corner without having an adventure. **[7]**

In the summer of 1982 Casey made *Hot Shots* for his friend Wakefield Poole, who appears to have been strapped for cash, until approached by Mustang Video's Toby Ross. But if Ross paid Casey well for his participation—$20,000, well aware that they would easily recover their investment—Poole was paid just one-tenth of this. The director explained:

With this movie, Hot Shots, *I became a pornographer. I'd never thought of myself as one because I'd always had other reasons for making a movie besides showing men have sex. It was always a learning experience. Something new. But this was different. I had nothing new to say. This film was just like any other movie: a setting, a situation, a hard-on, some sex, and an orgasm, shown from two different angles to make it appear eternal. Enough for some, and for now enough for me. I did it for money, not much of it, but we could at least eat well.* **[8]**

Poole was selling himself short. Though some of the scenes *are* fairly unadventurous those with Casey—

167

which link them together—are sublime, proving that at almost forty he has lost none of his magic. As the film opens we are unsure who John Sharp (Casey) is —what he does for a living to enable him to live in such opulent surroundings. The soundtrack is very Hollywood *film noir* as we see him arriving home in a Rolls-Royce driven a liveried chauffeur. Kissing his girlfriend goodnight, he enters his apartment and a large room containing just an ottoman and triptych mirror. Slowly and seductively, gazing from one reflection to another he removes his tuxedo, bow-tie and shirt. A screen appears above the mirrors, and Casey Donovan materializes, pleasuring himself. Reclining on the ottoman, the soundtrack changes to Debussy as John and his alter-image masturbate together. There are shades of *Casey* as he wakes up next morning, fixes himself breakfast, picks up the mail and takes it back to bed to read: promotional material for the *Hot Shots* film series. He gets into his bathtub and masturbates again, a process linking the scenes, until the final money shot. First off we see the boss, Rick Madison, dictating notes to his secretary as employees James Gallo and William Winer head off to the toilets to engage in mutual fellatio while colleague Richard Post leans against the wall, watching. Madison then takes Post back to his office and has sex with him on top of his desk. Next up, we see Louie Moscoso descending to the basement, where he is fellated by a leather-clad man he has chained to a chair. Some believed at the time

168

that this was Casey—he is wearing a leather head-mask and his face is not seen—but as his outfit is open at the front displaying no chest hair, whoever he is, it is *not* Casey. The camera then cuts to Philip Wagner and John Taylor, having fun in the back of the company limousine, and as this ends we return to Casey, standing up in the tub and delivering the money-shot.

It is only now that we find out who John Sharp is, as he put on his chauffeur's uniform, And is it really Casey crooning Elvis Presley's "You Were Always On My Mind" while getting ready for work? He then gets into the limo, picks up the boss, and he and Madison head for the latter's apartment to have sex—and we finally learn that it is his *hustling* that enables him to live in such luxury. Yet another masterpiece from Wakefield Poole!

In *Hot Shots*, subsequently retitled *Always Ready*, Casey's fans saw his tattoo for the first time—the initials "M. O." on his right outer thigh which until now had been concealed by make-up. At around this time he, Daniel Holt and rising star Rod Phillips (later the lover of Joey Stefano) were interviewed by author and activist Vito Russo for a NYC cable television documentary. Rejected for being too controversial, this was given a limited release by Bijou Video as *Men on Film: Too Hot for Cable*. In it, Casey explained what the initials "M. O." represented:

169

Office Master stands for a very hot pal of mine. He has about thirty-seven sexual slaves that he plays with. I was always his Number One. When I went to L. A. in 1980 to celebrate paying off one of the mortgages on my house in Key West, I decided I wanted to be his slave full time for three days. I gave him this tattoo as a present. (Shows the OM tattoo to the camera) This man is the most professional sexual person I have ever met, the most imaginative fantasy man. I can tell how he's taken a lot of people, including me, to a lot of interesting heights. He's very special. He's the hottest daddy in L A. **[9]**

In his biography of Casey, Roger Edmonson quotes *Manshots'* Robert Richards as having being told by Casey that one of Office Master's "slaves" was "an actor who had starred in one of the most wildly successful films of 1977." This *could* have been a reference to Christopher Reeve, with Casey getting the year wrong (*Superman* came out in 1978), but he was almost certainly another American star who, now as in 1998, cannot be named for legal reasons. Richards' quote concluded:

The man's career bottomed out in the early '80s but took off like a rocket about four years ago. Now he's on the top of the heap again. Cal loved the idea that he had the same S/M master as this guy. If he were alive today, he'd be ecstatic about the proxy celebrity of it all. **[10]**

170

In the spring of 1983, Casey achieved a dream that quickly turned into his worst nightmare. Reflecting upon where he had spent some of his happiest hours —in the New York bathhouses—he opted to revive *The Ritz*, Terrence McNally's farce which sees a straight Cleveland businessman, Gaetano Proclo, taking refuge from a mobster in a gay bathhouse in Manhattan where he finds himself thrown into a melee of oddball characters. These include squeaky-voiced detective Michael Brick, hammy Puerto Rican singer Googie Gomez, and the businessman's hyperactive wife who tracks him down and causes problems, assuming wrongly that he is secretly gay. Also on the bill were chubby-chasers and over-the-top camp go-go boys.

McNally, resident playwright at Yale University, had written *The Tubs* in 1974 and this had been presented by the university's Repertory Theatre before moving to Broadway's Longacre Theatre in January 1975, where the title had been changed to *The Ritz* owing to the popularity of Jerry Douglas' *Tubstrip*. The cast had included Jack Weston as Gaetano, Stephen Collins as Brick and, playing Googie, *West Side Story*'s Rita Moreno, who won a Tony Award for her performance. Moreno and Weston had revived their parts for the 1976 film, when Brick had been played by Treat Williams.

Casey and a director-producer friend, Michael Bavar, formed Bavar & Culver Productions. Bavar (1940-91) had staged a number of minor provincial productions, and in 1975 had penned a best-selling biography of Mae West. Each invested $100,000 in the venture—Casey's money coming mostly from hustling, an indication of how much wealthy clients

171

were willing to pay for his services as a stud, and how good he must have been if he could earn this much in the two months that it took to put the production together.

For their venture, Casey and Bavar chose Xenon, the Manhattan nightclub, at the time the only venue popular enough to compete with the more famous Studio 54. Among its regulars were Elton John, Robin Williams, Mick Jagger and Jerry Hall, Elizabeth Taylor, Liza Minnelli—and Casey's ex-lover Christopher Reeve. More glitzy than Studio 54, the walls were done out in silver, and a giant "X" attached to the ceiling projected rays of light on to the dance floor. The dress-code at was also more relaxed, with many patrons turning up in swimsuits and queuing to dance in the "go-go" boxes.

Whose decision it was to hire Holly Woodlawn for the pivotal role of Googie Gomez, made so memorable by Rita Moreno, is not known, but it would turn out to be a grave mistake. Woodlawn (1946-2015) was the Andy Warhol muse—born Haroldo Santiago Franceschi Rodriguez Danhakl in Juana Diaz, Puerto Rico, but brought up in Miami. Best known as the "he was a she" in Lou Reed's song, "Walk on the Wild Side", she had famously appeared in Warhol's *Trash* alongside the "Little Joe" in the song, Joe Dallesandro. Though always referred to as "she" and "transgender", Woodlawn confessed that though she had considered having reassignment surgery, she had never gone along with it—therefore, physically she was always a man. She was also extremely unreliable—a walking disaster who drank heavily and took drugs. Roy Blakey, hired by Casey to take the publicity photos,

172

remembered her as being "totally disorientated" throughout the session.

Woodlawn's irrational behaviour had become so bad by the time of the previews that Michael Bavar wanted to fire her and find a replacement. Casey talked him out of it, though he would soon wish that he had listened to his friend. The fact that much of the humour in *The Ritz* centered around Googie being persistently mistaken for a drag queen, when the actor playing her was effectively precisely this, brought guffaws of the wrong kind from audiences.

One of Casey's wealthier clients was the German-born socialite, banker and fashion designer Prince Egon von Furstenberg (1946-2004). Casey had first met him in Europe during his hustling tour, and they had frequently hooked up. It was he who organized the party for Casey and the cast in which took place in the auditorium after the play's premiere on 2 May 1983, where guests were given the choice to dress formerly—or to turn up wearing towels. Needless to say, many of Casey's gay fans chose the latter. The premiere proved a disaster. The critics—the ones who wielded enough power to close a play down after a single performance—hammered it, nothing to do with Casey or Woodlawn, but on account of the smaller parts and Michael Bavar's appalling direction. Lee Alan Morrow had already forewarned his readers in the previous week's *Back Stage*, after attending one of the previews:

> Frankly, it was impossible to differentiate what were supposed to be the intentionally bad performances from those that constituted someone's true efforts. Michael

173

Bavar, the director, treated the McNally script like a buffoon, grinding out cheap little jokes. The comedy was completely swamped by poor casting, poor staging, and nary an ounce of original interpretive thought. Rather than reviving *The Ritz*, Bavar and his colleagues buried it. [11]

Clive Barnes of *The New York Post* denounced the play as "undernourished, undercast and unfulfilled". *The New York Times'* Mel Gussow, who had hated the Broadway production of *Tubstrip* and who for reasons known only to himself loathed Casey with a vengeance—it is believed because he had once been a client, and was terrified of him outing him, which with his tendency towards extreme discretion would not have happened—was similarly unsparing:

> In dinner theatre, one dines and also sees a show. In disco theatre, one sees a show and then can stay to dance. While this is a money saver, the new production of "The Ritz" is no bargain. Of the three versions of the show I have seen, at the Yale Repertory Theater [*The Tubs*], on Broadway and at Xenon, this is easily the least amusing and the most overbearing. What made the show on Broadway were the performances of Jack Weston as the garbage man and especially Rita Moreno as Googie. While Taylor Reed fills the requirements of the former role, he is chubby and easily agitated and he lacks his predecessor's bedazzlement. Googie survives in our memory of Miss Moreno. In

174

the current production, the role is undertaken by Holly Woodlawn, a transvestite actor of Andy Warhol movie fame. He is not bad, but he is not Googie. As an actor pretending to be a woman who is mistaken for a man, he is far less funny, for example, than Julie Andrews was in almost the reverse situation [in *Victor, Victoria*]. A few of the actors keep the comedy from flagging, including Michael Greer as the camp queen of the frolic and Casey Donovan as the falsetto-voiced detective who tries to unravel the mistaken identities. The problem is not so much in any single performance as in the insistence of Michael Bavar's production, which is about as subtle as a wet towel. **[12]**

The fate of the play had virtually been decided by Terrence McNally when the curtain came down on the premiere, but the reviews the next day sounded the death-knell. Holly Woodlawn later said that it would have worked, had the cast been given more time to polish their performances. Casey too said that any first-night hitches would have been sorted by the second performance. Instead, he headed back to Key West and for several days shut himself away at Casa Donovan, convinced that his theatrical career—which he had hoped to revive now that he was about to turn forty and too old to continue with porn—was well and truly over.

Over the next six months, Casey zipped back and forth on his overseas tours, and found time to "help out" at the Red Barn Theatre, on Key West's Duval Street if ever they were lacking a leading man. He is known to have appeared in their production of *Boys in the Band*, and in *The Prime of Miss Jean Brodie*. In the autumn of 1983 he filmed the aforementioned interview with Vito Russo, and spoke about getting older:

> *I've always liked older men and wanted to be an older man myself. Early on I decided I wanted to keep it together. I'm glad that I've kept this promise to myself. I know about forty people who have died in the past two years. I don't do drugs or drink, and I'm working to keep myself healthy. I'm still working as a hustler through the pink pages of The Advocate. I think it's fabulous that people are still paying for it. Why the hell not? I tell you, I'm looking forward to fifty. I want to be a hot daddy!* [13]

Casey spoke of his plans for the future: a fitness and aerobics video, and four or five films during the next year, one of them to be directed by himself:

> *There must be some perverse joy that I get out of being a porno star. I was thinking the other day how many millions of gays there are in the U.S., but only hundreds have fucked on film. I guess I get off on that. I did* Boys *then one film after another came along and I've no idea what possessed me to keep on doing them, except that I'd become a recognisable commodity. Also I enjoyed the idea that I was doing something that very few people had ever done...Very interesting people wanted to meet me. Fabulous people*

176

wanted to do things for me....I think porno worked in my life because I was so honest about it. I treated it all very lightly....You have to have a sense of humour and treat the whole thing as a goof. Every day was like a party and I went along for the fun. **[14]**

On 2 November 1983, Casey turned forty, and in a self-penned magazine feature reflected not on his life as a stage actor and porn star, but as a traveller and tour guide:

I've climbed the Great Wall of China. I've climbed inside the Great Pyramid of Cheops. I've climbed to the top of the highest pyramid at Tikai in the lush tropical jungle of Guatemala. I've climbed the mystical Huaynu Picchu in Peru. Except for climbing down the embankment of the Canadian side Of Niagara Falls (to my mother's horror) to retrieve a dropped comb when I was five years old, I hadn't really visited any of our greatest natural wonders in my own America. **[15]**

The first of Casey's "daddy" films was *Split/Image*, directed by Wakefield Poole for Malexpress. His friend had again fallen by the wayside: there were financial problems, his father had recently died, and his lover Paul Hatlestad was terminally ill. Poole had turned to drugs. He had emerged from his ordeal wounded, but ready to continue with his career. And one of those who helped him "get it together" once more was Casey:

177

Cal and I were great together. We seemed to give each other what we needed to accomplish our goals. I had never had a friend like him before or since, as our relationship was built on total trust and respect. Also, it's strange to say, we were still both naïve. We saw the good side of things and refused to acknowledge the bad. That was our strength and allowed us always to see hope, something better just around the corner. [16]

The tagline for *Split/Image* was a double-entendre that said it all: "Covermen—See How They Shoot!" Wakefield Poole's first film shot on video, it opens with hirsute underwear model Nick Mauro posing for pictures in the studio before heading for the woods to have sex with Paul Irish, who looks like a good scrub might not go amiss. Watching is John Charles Williams. The camera then cuts back to the studio where Mark De Santos poses for pictures in his jockstrap before dreaming up a fantasy where he is out riding his bike. He falls off, and is helped by blue-eyed blond Steve Kaye, who takes him home and bathes him in the tub. This leads to them having sex and forming a daisy-chain with "Daddy" Casey, who may or may not be Steve's real father. Finally, back in the studio Nick Pastore poses in a swimsuit before hooking up with lanky blond Pat Allen to engage in a spot of nude swimming, and sex on a sun-lounger.

The sex scenes aside, *Split/Image* may have been typical porno fare as opposed to the excellence that Casey and Poole were used to, but it paved the way for what would be Casey's finest film in his later years: *Boys in the Sand II*, the sequel, thirteen years down the track, to the one that had launched his career. And once again, Wakefield Poole would be at the helm.

Casey's column in *Stallion* magazine received hundreds of letters every month.

Casa Donovan, Casey's Florida home.

As Michael Brick in *The Ritz*.

An ageing Holly Woodlawn revisits *The Ritz* in
2013, two years before her death.

Prince Egon von Furstenberg
was not the only "blue-blooded"
lover Casey met on his travels.

"Daddy" Casey!

11: *Boys in the Sand II*

I've waited a long, long time to experience this déja vu. For years Wakefield Poole and I have talked about doing this sequel—although I never anticipated that he'd repeat that sequence so exactly. (Casey)

In the spring of 1984, While Wakefield Poole was casting *Boys in the Sand II*, Casey made a most spectacular return to his "speciality"—porn feature films with the entire scenario built around his character, as opposed to an unrelated single scene. *Non-Stop* was directed by Steve Scott for Menexpress. Born Salvatore Grasso in New Jersey in 1937, Scott also acted, and had started his career in straight porn—throwing in the towel in the wake of *Deep Throat*, claiming that he would never be able to keep up with the competition. Scott had a fascination for filming the money-shots in slow-motion, and for uncircumcised or Latino actors such as Steve Collins, Jorge Rodriguez and Steve Peters, who appear here. He hated having canned music in sex scenes, which is why the action in the first half of the film eschews this for a television soundtrack. One of Al Parker and Jack Wrangler's favourite directors, he died in 1987, one month after Casey.

In the film, Steve Collins plays airline steward Steve Reynolds, who stops off between flights at his friend Jeff's Hollywood home for a lay-over. Instead of Jeff, he finds platinum blond Peter Wave asleep on the bed. Steve turns on the television: it is

182

an episode of *Legacy*, where we see his soap star buddy Dave Wilson (Casey) splitting up with his mistress after being with her on the show for five years. He calls Dave in New York, his next lay-over stop, and makes arrangements to stay at his apartment, then heads for the shower. In the meantime, Peter wakes up, makes his move on Steve as he is dressing, and they have sex. Next we see Steve arriving at Dave's place in New York, where he and his new lover (Steve Anthony) are asleep on top of the bed. He strips, gets on to the bed next to them, and when they awake the three have explosive sex, with the lover topping Steve while Dave tops him. The action then transfers to another bedroom overlooking Times Square, where Dave's producer, Matt (Eric Ryan) is getting a similar wake-up call from his production assistant lover, Gil (Daniel Holt). When they are done, Matt sends Gil on an errand—to deliver the latest script of *Legacy* to Dave. Gil and Steve make eye-contact, but nothing happens as Gil leaves, followed by Dave who has to go the studio. Steve stays behind, and glances out of the window to see Steve Peters sunbathing on the roof below and taking himself in hand. He does likewise while they watch each other. Next we see Dave in Matt's office, going over the script—then staring at his crotch and fantasising about them having sex, firstly on top of the table in the garage, then talking dirty while up against the painted stone wall before the vision ends and Dave returns to reality. In the next scene, Steve and Gil are in a clothing store. They cruise each other, and head for an abandoned building across the way, where they have sex as Mark Leonard watches from

183

the doorway. The film ends with Dave walking to the studio, and chancing upon handsome Latino, Jorge Rodriguez. Jorge offers an approving nod, and they descend to a basement where Dave proffers lip-service. "Man, I'm gonna be fucking late for work," he drawls as he zips up, and rushes across to the studio—after which we see Steve driving back to the airport, ready to start a new shift. All in all, an excellent film—one of Casey's finest and proof, if proof were needed, that at forty he still had that "it" factor that had been making fans go weak at the knees for thirteen years, a long time for any porn star to remain at the top of their profession.

The film was completed in June 1984, and within days Casey was preparing for the production which would see his career turning full-circle, with him and Wakefield Poole returning to where it all started—Fire Island. Earlier in the year, Pool had made *The Hustlers* with Steve Collins, who had gone straight into *Non-Stop* opposite Casey—and Casey's "son" Steve Kaye from *Split/Image*. Casey had watched the rushes for *The Hustlers*, and been taken up by arguably the most *un*attractive man in the production, Puerto-Rican Victor Houston. When Poole announced that he had gone into partnership with Malexpress producer Bill Adkins, and that they planned shooting *Boys in the Sand II*—with Casey heading the credits, naturally, Casey insisted that Houston appear in the film too.

Poole had decided that Casey would *not* be seen emerging from the sea in the sequel to *Boys in the Sand*, and auditioned twenty actors for this pivotal scene—according to one critic, a task as impossible as hiring someone else to play Maria von Trapp in a

184

remake of *The Sound of Music*. After a great deal of deliberation, he plumped for twenty-six-year-old Pat Allen, who had appeared in *Split/Image*, though not in a scene with Casey. At six-feet two inches, Allen would be the tallest of Casey's co-stars, and one of the most handsome. Born in Camp Pendleton, California, he had been raised in numerous military bases around America by his father, a major with the U.S. Marine Corps. Poole observed of his new star:

> *He was striking, tall, thin, and pleasant. He was also well-hung and, like Cal, versatile. He lacked only that Intangible substance that set "Casey" apart from the others. Still, he was the best around and thrilled to appear in the movie.* [1]

Shooting began on 20 August 1984, and the next day, Robert Richards interviewed Casey at great length for *Stallion* magazine. He observed:

> Casey Donovan is the real thing. Everybody knows him and everybody likes him. In a field where people are treated with all the respect of yesterday's newspapers, he's remained at the top for more than a dozen years. In the survival category that puts him in a class with Tina Turner or Norman Mailer....Sitting with him in the noonday glare, one notices he hasn't changed much since 1971 when the original *Boys in the Sand* shot Donovan to international renown—the years have been kind. [2]

185

Casey remarked of his "replacement":

> *I had no vision of losing my crown as 'King of Gay Porn'. It was wonderful watching young Pat do the scene—seeing him looking so much like me out there in the water. I see a great resemblance. It's almost eerie. We clicked the moment he walked into the office—instant rapport. I knew at once it was going to be fun!* [3]

Casey had spoken to Vito Russo of hoped for future film projects, including one about himself growing old gracefully as a porn star. He told Richards:

> *I still want to do the* Forty *film I was working on before I produced* The Ritz *on Broadway last year. There seems to be a need for that film. People who had heard I was working on it keep asking me when they can see it. Be patient, men! Soon—hopefully!* [4]

Of his longevity in a genre of film known for a swift turnover of actors, he observed:

> *A film or two and they vanish. In my case my life was made much more exciting by having made those films... Think of how ridiculous it is that I got involved in this. When I was modelling, I learned that you can work as long as you keep yourself looking good, and I always felt that my biggest successes would occur after forty, later in life.* [5]

Boys in the Sand II is an inspirational film, yet another with distinctive Beauty and the Beast elements—featuring the kind of sexual partner that Casey obviously preferred away from the screen, and the type of man the fans wanted to see him coupled with, one whose bullish unattractiveness highlighted Casey's still staggering good looks. It opens with a plane zooming overhead, and aerial shots of Fire Island. The camera zooms in on Casey, on his knees servicing beach bum Victor Houston in "The Meat Rack", the wooded area where he had coupled with Peter Fisk in the first film. The sex, however, does not replicate that in the first film. It is a rough, sweaty and noisy affair, with much of the dirty talk growled by Casey who, as in *Non-Stop*, persistently addresses each of his two lovers here as "Fucker". His facial expressions are priceless as, like before, he is completely oblivious to the camera. In thirteen years, he has changed but little as we watch him weave his magic on the balding Houston—a casual pick-up who receives a cursory handshake when they are done and go their separate ways. Casey returns home via the boardwalk and a jog along the shore, and finds an envelope pinned to the door. Inside is a piece of paper inscribed, "Bayside, Tomorrow, Six O'Clock." Thus he returns the next morning to the exact spot where Peter Fisk spread his sheet thirteen years ago—to witness vision of loveliness Pat Allen, running out of the water towards the shore. The sequence had to be filmed several times at six on a chilly morning—one take ruined because a boat sailed by, another because Pat became overcome with emotion upon reaching Casey on the

187

shore, and burst into tears on account of the emotion. Robert Richards, who kept a diary of the six-day shoot, curiously written in the present tense, reported, "Tenderly, Pat reaches down, kisses him, and whispers, 'Thank you for making this possible for me.'"

The scenario is the same as before, save that this time we have *two* stunning blonds going into the bushes not to have sex, but to *make love*, taking it in turns to top each other. Then, when they are done and have kissed goodbye, Casey rushes into the sea and disappears for ever, leaving Pat bewildered. The young man puts on Casey's discarded white pants and Hawaiian shirt and returns to the house. Next morning we see him despondently searching among the holiday crowds for his lost love, and at eventide gazing sadly across at the darkened ocean. Night comes, and he is in bed when he hears splashing outside in the pool. Here, in the moonlight, he finds an apparition which becomes real when he dives into the water and touches it. Paul Irish barely reaches past Pat's shoulders, but he is attractive, acrobatic and most splendidly endowed, wearing designer stubble and a cock-strap—and as with Danny DiCoccio in the original film does not climax during the sex scene. There was a reason for this—an attack of nerves—according to those watching, on account of Pat's massive orgasm, even more copious than the herculean one he produced during his scene with Casey. Indeed, claimed to have been the largest ever seen on a gay porn set, this caused *such* a fuss that Richards felt obliged to write an entire paragraph in his diary for *Stallion*:

Just before filming began, Pat told me he hadn't cum in four days. Now, as he approaches climax, the tension is incredible. He trembles, moans, writhes and erupts. Truly, *erupts*! He just keeps cumming and cumming, his cock bobbing and leaping, spewing out great waves of gism. Irish, shocked, moves back, watching in awe as Allen keeps on shooting. The crew is stunned—how can you tell the folks back home about this? Still it continues. A look of terror crosses Pat's face—he's never experienced anything like *this*! On and on it goes, until he collapses in a heap, his torso heaving, his blond head thrashing from side to side. No one can believe what they've just seen—and Pat can't believe what he's just done. Someone laughs, the tension is broken—work continues deep into the night.
[6]

The lovers dive into the pool, and Paul vanishes, leaving Pat lonely once more. Next morning, he is on the beach drinking a beer when blond bombshell Tony Williams strolls by with power-packed Dave Connors—who sadly took his own life before the film's release, having been diagnosed with AIDS. Dave gives Pat the eye, and fantasy takes over when Dave and Tony get home and have sex and Pat projects himself into the scenario, alternating replacing each of the two lovers. The camera moves between Dave being fellated by Pat while swinging from a gym-ring, then by Tony, and finally zips back and forth between him topping both men. The

189

fantasy ends with Pat back on the beach, glancing up as a shadow falls across his body. This is Dave, who pulls him to his feet, and they leave the beach arm in arm, walking off into the sunset.

Another visitor to the set was journalist Craig Rowland, who opined how Fire Island was no longer the romantic haven portrayed in Wakefield Poole's films, but a potentially dangerous location for today's gay man:

> A cloud hangs over this playground for the world's gay thoroughbreds, one of the symbols of the evolving upbeat self-fulfilment consciousness, and it isn't just the wretched weather of the '84 season when rain dampened the beach almost every weekend. A new and terrifying disease has settled over the gay community at large and continues to send shockwaves throughout the "movement" and the personal lives— directly or indirectly—of practically everybody who steps off the ferry in the Pines harbour or its neighbouring Cherry Grove, the other infamous resort that claims its gay identity back to the 1920s. Though the Pines and the Grove have become glorious retreats from the worries of the world, AIDS is one problem that can't be left at home with the business suit and mortgage payments. It is something that has insidiously entered our souls, travelling with us wherever we go. Some think the fire on Fire Island has been reduced to cinders because of it…But men continue to go there,

with lifestyle modifications heading the list on the itinerary. [7]

For now, few heeded such warnings and the team involved with *Boys in the Sand* had other problems, more pressing. The film had hit its first snag *before* the cameras started rolling. On the morning of the shoot, as Wakefield Poole was about to leave for Fire Island, he received a call from Bill Adkin's partner, Diane Pearlstein, informing him Adkins had succumbed to a fatal heart-attack. Poole was all for halting the shoot, but Pearlstein insisted that the production go ahead, in Adkins' memory. However, once the film was in the can, she changed her mind. Poole was told that she had sold the film outright to Los Angeles Video, and that his services were no longer required. He, however, held the upper hand, having given Pearlstein the transfer copies only, which had numbers running across the bottom for the editor, and as such were useless. Pat Allen also exacted his revenge on this contrary woman whose change of mind had resulted in him and the other actors not getting paid for their participation—while Casey had received his fee upfront. Pearlstein was a schoolteacher, but what her employers did not know was that she was running a male escort service on the side. Pat contacted *The New York Post*, which subsequently ran a front page headline, "Brooklyn Teacher's Secret Life in Escort Agency".

Casey's interview with Robert Richards appeared in a special issue of *Stallion* in January 1985, but it took eighteen months of acrimonious litigation before the film could be released, and with Poole compelled to purchase the rights from Pearlstein for

191

$8,000. Then, while attracting considerable praise, and in particular for Casey and Pat Allen's performances, there was criticism regarding the film's disregard for safe-sex. This was the middle of the Reagan-era AIDS crisis, and more had now been learned about the disease. Questions were also asked about Dave Connors suicide—the fact that he had been well aware of his HIV status when making the film, yet still had not used a condom.

Casey complained of feeling unwell in September 1985, when he returned to Miami. This has caused some to since believe that he was not merely HIV-positive but that he had developed full-blown AIDS. Some of the speculation derives from a paragraph in Wakefield Poole's comment when recalling what happened when he hired Pat Allen for the beach scene with Casey:

> *I didn't want it to appear that I was killing him off, but Cal said not to worry, a fitting end, should he never work again. I had so many mixed emotions. It was hard not to think back to the time when we were here shooting the first movie. At our location site there was another beached boat on shore in exactly the same place as before. It was a little surreal.* **[8]**

In fact, Casey was suffering from nothing more than a bad chill. *All* the actors had complained about the cold while shooting the film. It had been the end of the summer season, and whereas the sex scenes for the first *Boys* film had all been completed in single takes, this time it had been different. Poole recalled:

All the sections went well, Even the night scenes were great, though Pat and Paul Irish almost froze to death...How they kept their erections during that scene was amazing. Each time I yelled "Cut!" they'd run to the clothes dryer in the shed by the pool to warm up. It's a hot scene, and you'd never guess they were so uncomfortable. **[9]**

The most likely explanation for Casey's comment to Poole was that, as he had turned full circle with this film—and hit forty—he really was thinking of bringing the curtain down on his porn career and quitting while he was still in his prime. His tour work with Hanns Ebelsten was taking up more and more of his time, and offers to return on the stage were coming in. One particular project that interested him was *City Men*, said to have been a cross between *Tubstrip* with clothes, and Claire Booth Luce's *The Women*, which had been filmed in 1939 with Joan Crawford and Norma Shearer, and with gay director George Cukor at the helm. In this, writers Laurence Sevelick and Philip Blackwell had replaced the catty females with bitchy gay men—with Casey playing the male equivalent of the naïve Shearer character who is unaware of what her philandering husband is getting up to. This was scheduled to open at the end of the year, and Casey was about to fly for New York to discuss this with the writers when he switched on the television on 2 October and saw the news report that Rock Hudson had died of AIDS, aged fifty-nine. He was devastated. This was the third friend he had lost in six months. Besides Dave Connors, Val Martin had

193

died in April. Casa Donovan had also been put on the market. For the past year it had been running at a loss. Casey left the house in the hands of a real estate agent and flew to New York, where he met Sevelick and told him that he would not be doing the play, that he had more pressing personal matters to deal with.

Casey was now a fervent advocate for safe sex, and had eschewed the play for a cameo appearance, as a fake vice cop, in *Inevitable Love*, financed by a group of clinical psychologists who had recently founded Intelligence in Video. It is believed to have been the first safe-sex porn film, though today it is regarded as a curiosity. "I haven't done it with anything but my VCR," one character opines, while another poses, "Remember when sex was *fun*? Many viewers were also put off by the voice-over, warning them at the start of the film:

> *Some authorities believe there could be some risk from open-mouthed kissing or intercourse with condoms through accidental exposure to blood and semen. So check the check the latest information with an AIDS hotline or current gay publications.*

Intelligence in Video also hired Pat Allen, said to have been disappointed not to be partnered with Casey in any of his scenes. The film tells of college pals and wrestling enthusiasts Gary (Allen) and Hal (William L. Kane). Director Henry Mach's intention was to prove that sex could be good *without* taking risks. Unfortunately, no one seems to be having much of a good time. Gary and Hal grope

194

each other a lot during their wrestling bouts and even sleep in the same bed, but nothing ever happens between them. They leave college and while Hal graduates Gary goes into the Army—they stay in touch by exchanging letters. We see Hal at the gym, where he realises that he is gay after getting porn legend Jon King to spot him. They kiss, and have sex by way of King not penetrating him, but by shoving his penis between his thighs and performing frottage—Mach's first lesson in safe sex. Elsewhere, a drunken and supposedly straight Gary is being put through his paces by two Army buddies. One teaches him how to put on a condom, and when he passes out the other rapes him—the suggestion being that this is acceptable because the rapist has rubbered up. As in *Boys in the Sand II*, Gary/Pat Allen comes to in time to produce a most majestic orgasm, also realises that he is gay, and when dishonourably discharged from the Army decides to become a hustler! His first trick fellates him in a public bathroom—insisting of course that he wear a condom while he is blowing him. Next we see Hal playing strip poker with two graduates. "Gee, it's so great to find other gay guys," he exclaims, as instead of having sex they masturbate. The camera then returns to Gary, who is picked up by Casey. He wants a kiss, but when Gary refuses he tells him that he is a vice-cop, and that he will not arrest him he lets him have his way. Gary relents, unaware that this is Casey's modus operandi to avoid paying for tricks. In the next scene, Hal has found love in the form of gay activist Bob (Ken Diamond). Bob's idea of fun involves licking cream off each other's toes and testicles, and tickling each other with feathers, so needless to say they do not stay together long. Cut to Gary, now working in a garage and enjoying a circle jerk with colleagues— which, the voice-over says, is also a recognised safe-sex technique. When they are done, wary of telling them he is gay, he lets them coerce him into going out on the town for a spot of gay-bashing, and they bump into Hal, now living in the area. The other two attack Hal, Gary comes to his rescue, and love triumphs!

For two of actors in the film, Jon King and Philip Wagner, it was a case of lessons not being learned. Both succumbed to AIDS—Wagner in 1989, King in 1995. Marc Stevens, who appeared in Casey's next film, *Chance of a Lifetime*, committed suicide upon learning that he had the disease. Directed by John Lewis for Gay Men's Health Crisis, this has everyone practising safe sex, and this time there is penetration. Upon its release, the company put out a statement from Casey, along with photographs of his "rubbered-up" penis:

> *Like a lot of people, I used to think using rubbers was a bore. Now I know they're not only easy to use, they can save lives. I'm more and more surprised to find rubbers at the bedsides or in the pockets of most of the men I know. They're getting to be a lot more fun. So use a condom. It's good for you!* **[10]**

Casey's segment of the film was shot on 8 October. Two evenings later he caught up with Christopher Reeve backstage at New York's Circle in the Square Theatre. The occasion was the opening night

196

of *The Marriage of Figaro*—the stage play version of the Mozart opera. Reeve was playing Count Alvira, while the leads were Anthony Heald and Mary Elizabeth Mastrontonio. Casey's "date" was Wakefield Poole, who also accompanied him to the post-premiere party. It was Reeve, however, who sneaked out with him before this ended, to the hotel room which Casey had reserved for them earlier.

Because of a legal battle, the title of
the film was temporarily changed.

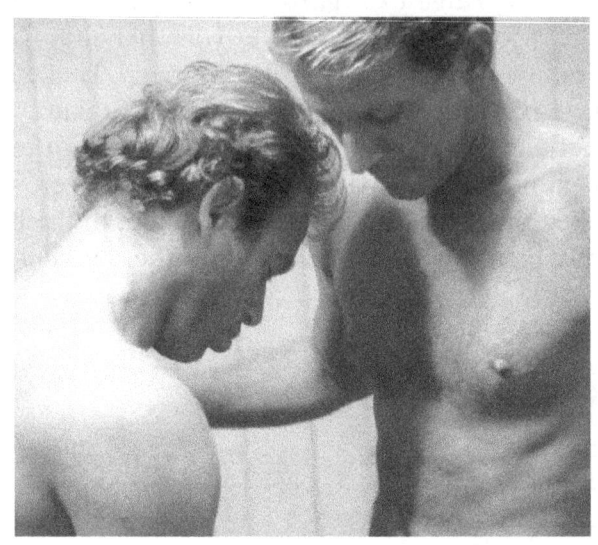

With Erik Ryan in *Non-Stop*.

Waiting for his mystery lover in *Boys in the Sand II*.

Pat Allen.

Posing between takes!

12: *The Last Sunset*

He revolutionised skinflicks by making the merely prurient psychologically probable by suggesting that the boy next door had all the stuff that erotic dreams are made of. (Martin Greif)

Casey spent the first half of 1986 working for Hanns Ebensten, escorting tours around the world—even as far afield as Australia, which proves that he must have been in sufficient good health to acquire travel insurance, and not suffering from the ravages of a terminal illness, as some have suggested. In the late summer of this year, he made what would be his last film: *Fucked Up* was directed by Christopher Rage. This comprised a "live" performance with John Clayton, who featured in just two films—the second would be in Joey Stefano's *Hard Steal*, ten years later. *Drummer*'s John F. Karr observed of the extreme scenario:

> Do you want to see a superstar get so turned on he becomes more of a sleazy animal than a human? Casey Donovan turns in an uninhibited, slutty performance only he could submit to. For one solid hour you'll watch Casey and his co-star John (he looks like he might be Casey's older brother...a very hot man) get nastier by the minute...By the end of this amazing hour he's thrashing on the bed moaning, "I want to get fucked, I want to get fucked!" It's sex-crazed, stoned out, piggy, nasty. And fucked up! [1]

Casey's swansong received some dreadful reviews, and hardly surprising. It opens with him having his bottom shaved with an electric trimmer, and during the ensuing scenario he does something which *never* occurred in his other films—he keeps glancing up at the cameraman, as if apprehensive over what is about to happen next, and realizing that he really *is* going too far this time. Physically, he has changed very little—the addition of a nipple-bar, and another through his navel. He is naked but for a white socks, and curiously wears what looks like a wedding-ring, while his bandana-wearing bed-partner is the one who looks ravaged, with a pock-marked face. The pair kiss, there is mutual masturbation and fellatio, after which the scenario becomes increasingly more puerile. Casey's facial expressions become half-crazed as he sniffs amyl nitrate from a jar, and the pair work their way through an assortment of dildos of all shapes and sizes, until Clayton pushes his fist into Casey's anus. One imagines it is not the kind of film that his fans would wish to watch more than once—that is, if they can stick it out until the end. Such a film was maybe only to be expected from Christopher Rage. *Manshots* called it, "A haunting study in self-destruct, a pathetic footnote to a glittering career, an unsettling record of the Golden Boy on a collision course with his own mortality." The un-named reviewer was not wrong.

It is not this author's intention to dwell on the last months of Casey's life and his final illness. Others have done this, often disrespectfully and without the slightest trace of decency. Mostly they have spoken retrospectively, unaware at the time that he *was* ill, inasmuch as others had related those fictitious tales

201

about his youth. It was as if some did not wish to remember Casey Donovan, pre-fame, unless as a perverted sexaholic—or in his final year as a shuffling, moribund shadow of his former shelf. He was criticised for having an "obsession" with memorial services, interpreted as him having been made aware that he himself might not have long to live. Nothing could have been further from the truth. Many of the men he had worked with professionally had died prematurely. By attending their funerals he was but showing his respect.

When Casey learned that his former teacher and mentor Helen Van Fleet was retiring, he travelled to Canandaigua and was mobbed by fans and friends at his former school. Everyone was aware that the Calvin Culver they had known all those years ago had become one of the world's top porn stars, but it made not one jot of difference. At a concert held in Helen's honour—announced as "Patrick", her pet name for him—he sang a parody of her favourite song from *Mame*. In the April, photographer Roy Blakey bumped into him in a New York street, and described him as "looking more gorgeous than ever, seemingly immune to the ageing process."

So-called friends Robert Richards and Casey's former roommate Jake Getty were especially cruel towards his memory, mocking him for his spiritual stance—misinterpreting this for something much more sinister. His final tour with Hanns Ebensten took place in July 1987, when they visited Canada. Ebensten spoke of the one prior to this, in the May, when they had toured the Amazon basin and the guests had gasped in wonder as Casey had emerged from the hotel pool. "He was tanned and fit, and glowed with health," he said. Of his spirituality, he recalled trips they had made to Peru and Egypt:

> *He was mystic and very spiritual, so that he contrived to be alone in the Inca city at Machu Picchu at night in order to meditate...and when he climbed with our group down the thousands of rock-hewn steps from Mount Sinai one Thanksgiving Day, which happened also to be my birthday, and a strange white bow appeared suddenly in in the clear sky and dipped down directly into the Monastery of Saint Catherine in the valley below, he took this for a heavenly sign and stood in awe, then quickly captured the phenomenon with his camera and later named his photograph "The Miracle of the Sinai".* [2]

Wakefield Poole saw him for the last time at the end of July and observed that he looked great—"dressed up, buttoned down, the scent of woodsy soap clinging to him." He told me:

> *He knocked on my door and upon opening it I was surprised at what I saw. He looked wonderful and I was so relieved. I had heard how bad he looked and how low he'd sunk. None of that was evident. Mostly, he looked healthy. We had a cup of tea and talked briefly. He asked for some money and I gave him what cash I had on hand. I didn't ask why he needed it. We kissed at the door, and*

203

I watched him until the elevator doors closed. I heard from Jerry Douglas that he left for Florida two weeks after his visit. I love him and owe him so much. [3]

Casey had planned another tour of Egypt for Hanns Ebensten, to take place at the end of July, but gave backword—saying he had a bad chest and that the sand might make this worse, but still giving no one cause for concern. The first sign that he was very ill came on Thursday, 6 August, when he left New York for Inverness, Florida, where his parents now lived. He was taken to the plane in a wheelchair and, when this reached its destination transported by ambulance the 300 miles to the Citrus Memorial Hospital, in Inverness. He was finding it hard to breathe, and the doctors took tests, like Casey suspecting that he might have picked up something during his last trip to the Sinai. Hanns Ebensten called him on the Saturday:

> *He said that he was feeling well but that the doctors had found "a lot of white spots, like a snowstorm," on the X-rays of his lungs. We talked for some time, then he said he was very tired: "Bye, love you."* [4]

The following afternoon, Casey lapsed into a coma, from which he would not emerge. The next morning —Sunday 10 August—his parents were sitting at his bedside when he slipped away.

Epilogue

At no point during Casey's illness was the AIDS word mentioned—neither by the doctors at the Citrus Memorial Hospital, nor by his family. His friends and members of the press *assumed* that this had been the cause of his death, bearing mind that many of those he had worked with had succumbed to the disease. Unlike Freddie Mercury, Rudolph Nureyev and Rock Hudson—who looked emaciated and desperately ill towards the end of their lives—the last photographs of Casey reveal him as looking hale and hearty, with a slight paunch and receding hairline, but certainly not moribund. The Polish film director Richard Boleslavski (who made *The Garden of Allah* with Marlene Dietrich) and French heartthrob actor Gérard Philipe both died suddenly just weeks after working in desert locations similar to the one Casey had recently visited, so there is no reason to believe that his death was not attributed to a malady picked up in foreign parts. His death-certificate stated that he had died of "acute pulmonary infection resulting from respiratory deficiency", hence the white spots on his lungs.

"In other words, AIDS," Bob Stanford observed in *In Touch*, sparking off a rumour which persists to this day. This was the journalist jumping to the most obvious conclusion. There was *no* reference to weight loss in the medical report, *no* mention of Kaposi's sarcoma, or any other symptoms normally associated with the disease. Therefore there is every chance that Casey really *had* picked up a nasty infection while in Egypt, and that this took his life.

Casey's memorial service took place at a church in New York's Greenwich Village, with Helen Van Fleet leading the mourners. Prior to this there had been a private funeral in East Bloomfield, attended by family members and friends from his youth, followed by cremation. The tributes were legion.

Holly Woodlawn, his co-star in *The Ritz*, wept as she told the crowd, "He was the most gracious man I have ever encountered."

Jake Getty said, "He would go out of his way to do nice things for you. My friend Cal Culver was a Christian gentleman." Roy Blakey added, "Cal was one of the sweetest people on the face of this earth. He seemed untouched by the porn world he was part of. He was dazzling."

Michael Kearns, who appeared in *L. A. Tool & Die* and toured with Casey in *Tubstrip*, said, "Cal had star quality. He wasn't a whore, he was a courtesan. I loved him as an individual, and for the impact he had on the gay community. He did a great deal to liberate us and our sexuality from shame, and to bring gays out of the shadows into the light of day." Kearns also paid tribute to his friend in the Los Angeles weekly, *Edge*:

> *If not a great actor, he was a luminous presence on celluloid. Like all true film stars, he essentially portrayed himself: all-American, liberated, carefree. Even in his later films, as he aged and his onscreen sexual escapades became harder core, he maintained an impenetrable innocence. He never appeared jaded or tired: the Image prevailed.* [1]

Another friend, Jay McKenna, eulogised Casey in the *Los Angeles Update*:

> *His memory isn't obscured by false nostalgia. Cal had star power. He celebrated his gayness. He made me and others proud to be gay, so contagious was his spirit. To be in his presence was to breathe a rarified atmosphere.* **[2]**

Seven months after Casey's death, it emerged that his last wishes had been to have his ashes scattered on Fire Island. Why the Culvers had kept this information to themselves is not known, though they came good in the end and sent his ashes to Jake Getty. The ceremony took place on Monday, 4 April, where Calvin Culver's remains were returned to the spot he had loved, and which had brought him world fame. He truly was unique.

The last word will be left to Casey himself, who had told Vito Russo four years earlier:

> *I think my greatest accomplishment so far is something that doesn't show up in lights or get reviewed, and that's simply the sexual sanity that I've tried to contribute to over the past twenty years. I have never done anything to make a sick society any sicker. I've tried to be honest, kind and understanding with as many different people as possible, and I think that's much more important than just being gay. My goal is to live each day to the fullest.*

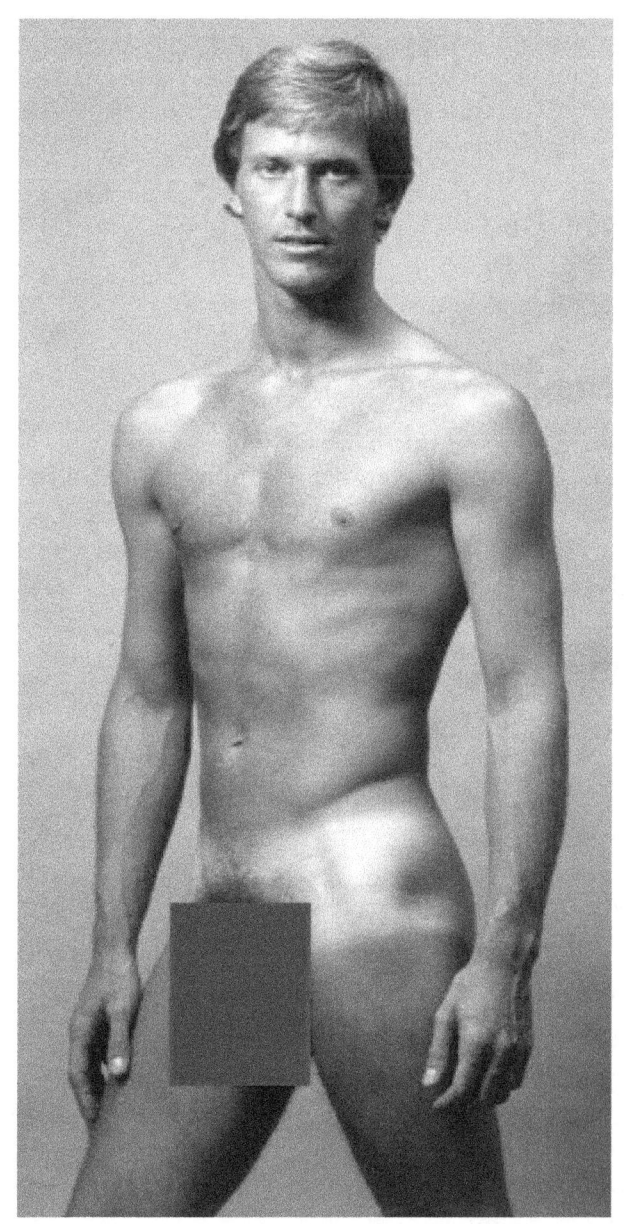

209

Filmography

Note: the dates are release dates, and not always when the films were made.

Twin Beds (1969)
Doctor X (1969)
Heterosexual loops. No more details.

Eleana
(AFDC, 1970)
Director/Script: Seemore Doules. Photography: Savas Kalogeras. With Athena Prezaki, Lisa Vern. Casey, in a heterosexual role, was billed as J. Calvin Culver. 59 mins.

Ginger
(Ginger Productions, 1971)
Director/Script: Don Schain. Photography: R Kent Evans. Music: Robert G. Orpin. With Cheri Caffaro, Duane Tucker, Herbert Kerr, David Ross. Michele Norris. Casey (billed as Calvin Culver) played Rodney Allworth. 90-102 mins, depending on print.

Casey
(Hand in Hand Films, 1971)
Director: Donald Crane. Script: Glenn Jones. Photography: Ron Almero. Music: Cyril Murnford. With Angelo Waine, Nat Grey, Sparrow Guano. Casey, originally billed as Ken Donovan, played himself. 82 mins.

Some of My Best Friends Are...
(Bluebird Productions, 1971)
Director/Script: Mervyn Nelson. Photography: Tony Mitchell. Music/Songs: Gordon Rose. With Sylvia Syms (singer), Candy Darling, Rue McClanahan, Uva Harden, Tom Bade, James Murdock. Casey (uncredited, listed on the call-sheet as Calvin Culver) played "a self-loathing hustler". 105 mins.

Dragula
(Moss Films, 1971)
Director/Script: Jim Moss. Photography: Andy Milligan. With Joe Downing, Calvin Holt, Jan Wallman, John Wallowitch, Hal Borske. Casey (billed as Calvin Culver) played Dracula's Son #1. 80 mins.

Boys in the Sand
(Poolemar, 1971)
Director/Script/Photography: Wakefield Poole. Music: Debussy. With Peter Schneckenberger (billed as Peter Fisk), Danny DiCiccio. Tommy Moore, Ed Parente (non-sexual role). 90 mins.

Pornography in New York
(Alpha Blue, 1972) Documentary
Director: Beau Buchanan. Script: Reveis Philmore III. Photography: Clyde Schwartz. Narrator: Ron Delaney. With Barbara Grumet, Gene Connolly, Lloyd Kaufman, Kim Lewd, Nancy, Carlos Tobalina. Casey appears as himself. 65 mins.

The Back Row
(Hand in Hand, 1973)

Director/Story: Doug Richards (Jerry Douglas): Photography: unknown, Music: William Cox. With George Payne, Robin Anderson, David Knox, William Carlton, Robert Tristan, Arthur Grisham, Chris Villette, Duane Colglazier (non-sexual). Casey is believed by some to have performed the songs on the soundtrack.

Fun and Games (UK: It Ain't Easy)
(Jaco Productions/Audobon Films, 1973)

Director/Script: Mervyn Nelson. Music: Gordon Rose. With Alice Spivak, Bob Hodge, Naomi Riis, Roxie Graziano. Casey (billed as Calvin Culver) played Bob Cartwright. 80 mins.

Erotikus: A History of Gay Movies
(Hand-in-Hand, 1973) Documentary

Director/Script: L. Brooks (Tom De Simone). Choreography: Tu L'Fete. Music: Amyl Nitrate. Narrator: Fred Halsted. With Billy Hitchcock, Glen Corbit, D.C. Michaels, Poco Allen, Ed Fury, Gary Conway, Larry Dancer, Monte Hansen, Voldemar, Myona Phetish, Ruffin Tumble, Sky Kink. Casey appears in a scene from *Boys in the Sand*. 85 mins.

Score
(Audobon Films, 1974)

Director: Radley Metzger. Script: Jerry Douglas. Photography: Frano Vodopivec. Costumes: Doris Toumarkine. Music: Robert Cornford. Song, "Where Is the Boy" performed by The Croatian Trio. With Claire Wilbur, Lynn Lowry, Gerald Grant, Carl Parker. Casey (billed as Calvin Culver) played Eddie. 83 mins, regular version. 90 mins, hardcore version.

Moving
(Poolemar Productions, 1974)

Director/Script/Photography: Wakefield Poole. With Burt Edouards, Val Martin, Curt Gerard, Peter Fisk, Tom Wright. 55 mins.

The Opening of Misty Beethoven
(Crescent Films/Audubon Films 1976)
Director/Script: Henry Paris (aka Randy Metzger). Photography: Paul Glickman (aka Robert Rochester). Music: George Craig. With Constance Money, Jamie Gillis, Jacqueline Beudant, Gloria Leonard. Casey played Jacques. 85 mins.

The Other Side of Aspen
(Falcon Studios, 1978)
Director/Script: Bill Clayton. Photography: Colin Myer. With Al Parker, Jeff Turk, Chad Benson, Dick Fisk, Mike Flynn (non-sexual). 35/39 mins. Note: the original longer, silent print is said to contain a fisting scene between Casey and Parker, which was cut when the sound version was being edited.

Gal Young Un
(Nunez Films, 1979)

Director/Script/Photography: Victor Nunez. Based on a short story by Marjorie Kinnan Rawlings. Costumes: Allen Eggleston. Music: Charles Engstrom, played by the Azalea Blosson String Band. With Dana Preu, David Peck, Gene Densmore, Mike Garlington, Tim McCormack. Casey (billed as Calvin Culver in the film credits, as Casey Donovan on the DVD release) played Jeb Langtry. 105 mins.

L. A. Tool & Die
(Joe Gage Films, 1979)

Director/Script: Tim Kincaid (aka Joe Gage). Photography: Richard Youngblood. Music: Al Steinman. Harmonica solos: Chuck Thatcher. With Richard Locke, Michael Kearns, Derrick Stanton, Joseph Kearns, Bob Blount, Joe Walsh and others. Casey played the part of Fred. 86 mins.

Heatstroke
(Gagefilm Productions, 1982)
Director/Script: Joe Gage. Photography: Russell Ballard. Music: Man Parish: With Richard Locke, Clinton Coe, Roy Garrett, Clay Russell, Bud Wallace, Richard West, John Steele, Bob Shane, Suzanne Tyson. Casey played Marty King. 88 mins.

Sleaze
(HIS Video, 1982)
Director/Script: Christopher Rage. Photography: Christopher Rage/Arch Brown. With Scorpio, Jed Black, Daniel Holt, Robert Castro, Antonio Feliz, Christopher Rage, Manuel Rodriguez, David Stoner. 75 mins.

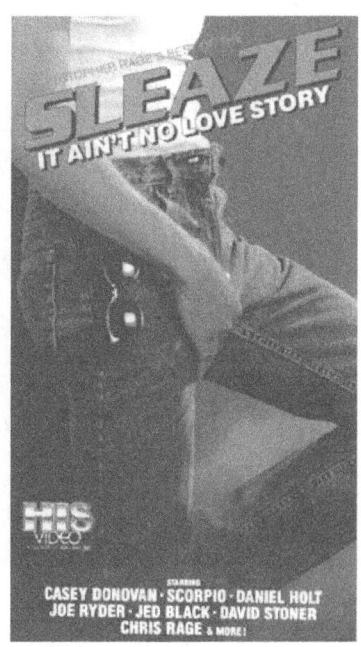

Christopher Rage's Superstars
(HIS Video, 1982)
Director/Script: Christopher Rage. Photography: Christopher Rage/Arch Brown. With George Payne, Scorpio, Richard Locke, Jed Black, Lee Marlin, Christopher Rage, Scott Taylor. 85 mins.

Hot Shots (aka Always Ready)
(Mustang Video, 1982)
Director/Script: Wakefield Poole. Photography: Wakefield Poole/Toby Ross/Ed Bennett. Music: Richard Bone. With Lou Davis, James Gallo, Rick Madison, Louie Moscoso, Philip Wagner, William Winer, John Taylor, Carrie Reynolds (non-sexual). Casey played John Sharp. 65 mins.

Split/Image (aka Double Hung) (Malexpress, 1984)

Director/Script/Photography: Wakefield Poole. With Pat Allen, Steve Kaye, John Charles Williams, Justin Savage, Mark DeSantos, Nick Mauro, Paul Irish, Nick Pastore. 90 mins.

Non-Stop (Malexpress, 1984)

Director/Script: Steve Scott. Photography: Tom Howard. With Steve Collins, Eric Ryan, Peter Wave, Daniel Holt, Steve Anthony, Steve Peters, Jorge Rodriguez. 78 mins.

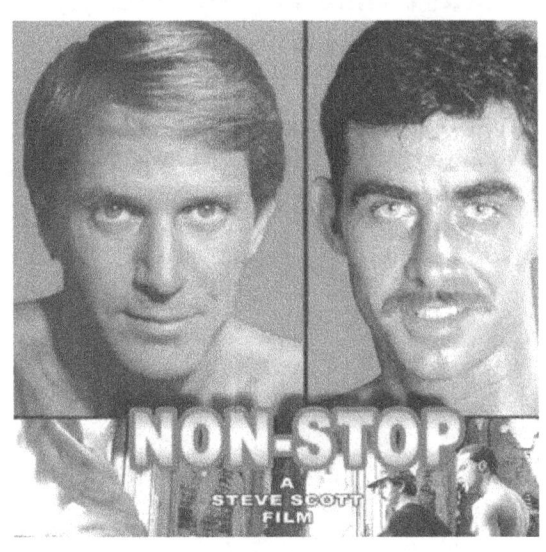

Boys in the Sand II (aka Men in the Sand)
(Real Time Productions, 1984)*
Director/Script/Photography: Wakefield Poole. With Pat Allen, Paul Irish, Victor Houston, Dave Connors, Tony Williams. 63 mins.
*released 1986.

Inevitable Love
(Intelligence In Video, 1985)
Director/Script: Henry Mach. Photography: Cyril Yanno. Music: The Bytebeat. With William Kane, Pat Allen, John King, Dwan, John Vernon, Jamie Wingo, Luke, Rich Carrone, Fred Gormley, Wolfe, Prince Pannece. Casey played "Fake Vice Cop", 90 mins.

Chance of a Lifetime
(Gay Men's Health Crisis, 1985)
Director/Script: John Lewis. Photography unknown.
With Gerald Campbell, Fred Gormley, Westbrook
Pegler, Dwight Hall, Eddy LaRosa, Marc Stevens,
Nolan White. 42 mins.

Fucked Up
(Live Video Inc., 1986)
Director/Script/Photography: Christopher Rage.
With John Clayton. 61 mins.

Theatre Productions

Pins & Needles (1967)
(New York, Roundabout Theatre)
Music & Lyrics: Harold Rome. Director: Gene Feist. Sketches: Joseph Schrank. Choreography: Larry Life. Costumes: Rose Federin. With Zaida Coles, Loretta Long, Joe Abramski. 214 perfs. Casey (listed on the call-sheets as John Calvin Culver) was a member of the chorus.

And Puppy Dogs' Tails (1969-70)
(New York, Bowerie Lane Theatre)
Written by David Gaard. With George Reeder, Tommy Spencer, Ken Kliban, Edward Dunn. 141 perfs. Casey (billed as Calvin Culver) understudied Edward Dunn who was frequently indisposed.

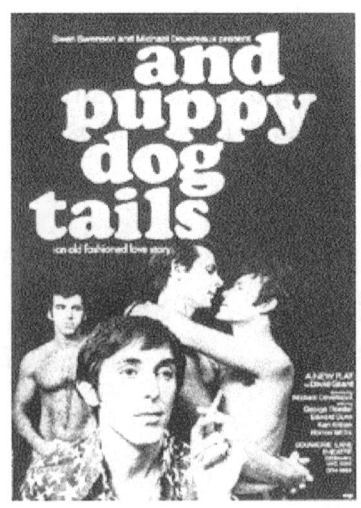

222

Brave (1970)
(New York, ANTA Theatre)
By Joseph Golden. Director: Tony Tanner. 6 perfs.

Circle in the Water (1970)
(New York)
Written, produced, directed by Jerry Douglas. With Ted Wuerffell. 24 perfs. Casey (billed as Calvin Culver) played Lieutenant Gregg Chandler.

Captain Brasshound's Conversion (Tour + New York, Ethel Barrymore Theatre)
Written by George Bernard Shaw. Director: Stephen Porter. Sets: Michael Annals. Costumes: Sara Brook. With Ingrid Bergman, Pernell Roberts, Eric Berry. Casey (billed as Calvin Culver) was "Sailor", "American Armed Guard", and understudied "Blue Jacket". The play toured Wilmington, Washington and Toronto before giving 16 perfs in New York.

The Merchant of Venice (1973)
(New York, Vivian Beaumont Theatre)
Written by William Shakespeare. Director: Ellis Rabb. Sets: James Tilton. Costumes: Ann Roth. With Philip Bosco, Rosemary Harris, Christopher Walken, Sydney Walker. Casey (as Calvin Culver) played Jesus Christ, and understudied the part of Leonardo. 44 perfs, including previews.

Tubstrip (1973-4)
(Tour +New York, Mayfair Theatre)

Writer: A. J. Kronengold (Jerry Douglas). Director: Jerry Douglas. Sets: Leo B Meyer. Costumes: Jim Faber. With Gerald Grant, Michael Kearns, A. J. D'Agostino (Casey's understudy), Jade McCall, Rick Cassidy, Walter Holiday, Jake Everett, Edward Rambeau, John Bruce Deaven, Dick Joslyn, Tam Van Stitzel. The play toured Los Angeles, Boston, Toronto, Detroit, Chicago and San Francisco (an estimated 500 performances) before giving 25 performances (including previews) in New York.

The Ritz
(New York, Xenon, 1983)

A Bavar & Culver Production in association with James R. Cunningham. Writer: Terrence McNally. Director: Micahel Bavar. Choreography: Robert Speller. Sets: Gordon Micunis. Costumes: George Potts. Music: Man Parrish. With Holly Woodlawn, Taylor Reed, Pi Douglas, John Burke, George Sardi, Danny Dennis, Dolores Wilson, Jon Koons, Paige Edwards, Tom Terwilliger, Jan Meredith, Michael Greer, Joey Faye, Don Potter, Roland Rodriguez, Peer Radon. Casey played Michael Brick. 14 previews in April. One performance 2 May 1983.

The Prime of Miss Jean Brodie/The Boys in the Band
(Key West, Red Barn Theatre, 1983)

Casey is known to have stood in several times during the summer months when his local theatre were short of a leading man. No further details.

Source Notes & Bibliography

Chapter 1
1: Leopold, Allan: "Calvin Culver, Lookin' Up", *In Touch*, July 1974
2/3: Leopold, ibid.
4: Turan, Kenneth & Zito, Stephen: *Sinema: American Pornagraphic Films and the People Who Make Them*, Praeger, 1974.
5/6/7: Leopold, ibid. Note: the editorial has Casey saying "last October", suggesting that the trip to Amsterdam had taken place in 1973, when he had been touring the United States with *Tubstrip*. This was an error, when what he had actually said had been "*that* October", referring to 1968. The Brel musical opened on the 4th of this month, and the Nureyev premiere on the 10th.
8: (Leopold, ibid, reaffirmed in his 1977 television interview with Frank O'Dowd for *Emerald City*).
9: Burrero, Romain: *Homosexual Renaissance*: 25 February 1970.
10: Leopold, ibid.
11: McClelland, Doug: *Filmograph*, 1972.
12: Douglas, Jerry: "Legend of Casey Donovan", *Manshots*, April 1992.

Chapter Two
1/2/3: Turan & Zito, ibid.
4: McClelland, ibid.

Chapter Three
1: Poole, Wakefield: *Dirty Poole: A Sensual Memoir*, Lethe Press, 2011.

2: Fritscher, Jack: "Dirty Poole: Everything You Fantasised About Porn Director Wakefield Poole But Were Too Wrecked to Ask", *Drummer*, 2/79

3: When one watches Wakefield Poole's original footage of *Bayside* with Fisk and Dino, one instinctively realizes what a vast change to gay porn was made by the appearance of Casey Donovan, and comes to the conclusion that without him, the project would have almost certainly been assigned to oblivion. Dino *clobbers* out of the ocean. He is bulky, ungainly, pleasantly-endowed, but has a flabby backside, an unruly mop of black hair, and a huge moustache—pretty much the kind of man who was appearing in crude loops at the time, and a direct contrast to the clean-cut, fresh-faced and almost innocent-looking Casey. His climax, when it occurs, is fake—quite obviously hand-cream—and when he and Peter Fisk are done having sex, it is *Dino* who runs back into the sea.

4: Leopold, ibid.

5: Canby, Vincent: *The New York Times*, 28/10/71.

6: Poole, ibid.

7: *Boys in the Sand* reviews, January-March 1972.

8: Fritscher, ibid.

9: Helms, Alan, *Out* magazine, January 2003.

10: Richards, Robert, "Our Gay Heritage: The Original *Boys in the Sand*," *Stallion*, January 1985.

Chapter Four

1: Leopold, ibid.

2: Jerry Douglas quote from the 2001 DVD release.

3: Payne, George: *The Advocate*, April 1973.

4: Interviewed by *The Rialto Report* in March 2013, Payne—probably defending his later reputation as a stud in heterosexual adult movies—claimed that Casey's climax was faked, much as had happened in *Casey*, but one only has to watch the sequence to see that it was not.

5: Baron, Adam: "Jerry Douglas Interview", *The Sword*, August 2014.
6: Jerry Douglas quote from the 2001 DVD release.
7: Turan & Zito, ibid.
8: Harris, Daniel: *The Rise & Fall of Gay Culture*, Hyperion, 1997.
9: Kramer, Gary: Interview with Radley Metzger, *Cinedelphia*, January 2014.

Chapter Five

1: Bowen, Michael: Interview with Lynn Lowry, on the restored release of the DVD.
2: Anonymous: *In Touch*, July 1974.
3/4: Burrows, Roberta: *After Dark*, July 1972.
5: Como, William: *After Dark*, July 1972.
6/7: Donovan, Casey: Speaking to William Como in Rome, June 1972, subsequently published in *After Dark*, July 1972.
8: Russo, Vito: *Men & Film*, TV documentary with Russo, Rod Phillips and Daniel Holt, 1983.
9/10: Turan & Zito, ibid.
11: *Newsweek*, 27 November 1972.
12: Turan & Zito, ibid.

Chapter Six

1: "Mr. Breckinridge", *The Thomas Tryon Tragedy*, December 2007.
2: Donovan, Casey: to Robert Richards, April 1973.
3: Barnes, Clive: "Stage: Modern Venice", *The New York Times*, 5 March 1973.

4: Symon, John: *New York Magazine*, 19/3/1973.
5: Turan & Zito, ibid.
6: Leopold, ibid.
7: Turan & Zito, ibid.
8: Baker, Robb: *After Dark*'s, May 1973.
9: —— —— to David Bret, February 2017.
10: *Los Angeles Times*, 30 September 1973.
11: Moriarty, J: *The Advocate*, November 1973.
12: Fairbanks, Harold: *The Advocate*, November 1973.
13: Jake Getty, quoted in Edmonson, p 141.
14/15: Poole, ibid.
16: King, Bruce: *Variety*, 8 August 1973.
17: Collins, William B: *Philadelphia Inquirer*, 2/74.
18: Anonymous: *Philadelphia Inquirer*, 2/74.
19: Whittaker, Herbert: *Toronto Globe & Mail*, March 1974.
20: Anonymous: "Tubstrip: A Play For Posterity?" *Detroit Free Press*.
21: Leonard, Will: "Brainless Gay Farce Fizzles", *Chicago Tribune,* 10 April 1974.
22: Donovan, Casey: *Viva,* June 1974.
23: Leopold, ibid.
24: Richards, ibid.
25: Gussow, Mel: *The New York Times*, 11/74.
26: Anonymous: *Oakland Tribune*, 2/11/74.

Chapter Seven

1: Richards, ibid. The affair with Reeve was also referred to by Darwin Porter and Danford Prince in *Hollywood Babylon Strikes Again* (Blood Moon, 2010) and by Casey, omitting Reeves' name, in a number of later interviews.
2: Anonymous: *The Advocate*, April 1976.

3: Douglas, Jerry: "The Legend of Casey Donovan", *Manshots*, April 1992.
4: Richards, Robert: *Manshots,* September 1978.
5: Chuck Holmes to Jerry Douglas, *Manshots*, 2/93.
6: Escoffier, Jeffrey: *Bigger Than Life: The History of Gay Porn Cinema*, Avalon, 2009.

Chapter 8
1: "Interview With a Legend", *Manshots*, 8/92.
2: Escoffier, ibid.

Chapter Nine
1: Plunkett, Robert: Interview with Hanns Ebensten, *The Advocate*, July 2000.
2: Ebensten, Hanns: *Volleyball with the Cuna Indians and Other Gay Travel Adventures.* Viking/Allen Lane 1993.
3/4: Ebensten, ibid.
5: Donovan, Casey: *Letters to Casey*, response, *Stallion*, January 1985.
6: Ebensten, ibid.
7: *Sleaze*: original box tag-line, 1982.

Chapter Ten
1/2: Richards, ibid.
3: Douglas, Jerry: *Manshots*, 1992, ibid.
4: Bret, David: *Joey Stefano*, DbBooks, 2016.
5/6/7: Richards, ibid.
8: Poole, ibid. The film was subsequently released under the title, *Always Ready*.
9: Donovan, Casey: *Men on Film: Too Hot for Cable*, 1983 aborted television documentary.
10: Richards, ibid.
11: Morrow, Lee Alan: *Backstage*, April 1983.

12: Gusso, Mel: *"The Ritz*, Farce", *The New York Times*, 2 May 1983.
13/14: *Men on Film*, ibid.
15: Donovan, Casey: "Letters to Casey" response, *Stallion*, later published in January 1985.
16: Poole, ibid.

Chapter Eleven

1: Poole, ibid.
2/3/4/5: Richards, Robert: "Casey Donovan: Going Strong at 40", *Stallion*, January 1985.
6: Richards, Robert: *"Boys in the Sand II* diary", *Stallion*, January 1985.
7: Rowland, Craig: "Fire Island Revisited", *Stallion*, January 1985.
8/9: Poole, ibid.
10: Donovan, Casey: Statement c/o Gay Men's Health Crisis, January 1986.

Chapter Twelve

Epigram by Martin Greif, *The Gay Book of Days*, The Main Street Press, 1982.
1: Karr, John F: *Drummer.*
2: Ebensten, ibid.
3: Wakefield Poole to David Bret, May 2017.
4: Ebensten, ibid.

Epilogue

1: Kearns, Michael: *Edge*, August 1987.
2: McKenna, Jay: *Los Angeles Update*, August 1987.

Printed in the USA
CPSIA information can be obtained
at www.ICGtesting.com
LVHW021117211124
797256LV00008B/212